A Daily Gift of

Hope

A COLLECTION OF STORIES FROM
HOPEFUL HEARTS AROUND THE GLOBE

Teresa Velardi

Interior Design by Amit Dey

Spirit Book Endeavors
c/o Authentic Endeavors Publishing
Clarks Summit, PA 18411

A Daily Gift of Hope
ISBN: 978-1-955668-80-4 (Paperback)
        978-1-955668-91-0 (eBook)

*Hope is the word which God has written
on the brow of every man.*

Victor Hugo

The lighthouse is the beacon of hope for sailors lost at sea.
Let your light shine ... it's hope for those around you!

Dedication

*T*his book is dedicated to:

The memory of Michelle J Patterson, a beacon of light and hope for so many women. Her strength and endurance were unmistakable and unmatchable.

Keep dancing with Jesus, my friend.

The memory of Abel Isaac, whose short time on earth filled the hearts of so many people. His light-filled purpose shines brightly through his family and the books his mom creates in his name. You were undoubtedly *Born Abel*, little one.

And all those who have ever felt hopeless.

May love and hope fill your hearts no matter your challenges.

Hope smiles from the threshold of the year to come,
whispering 'it will be happier.'

Alfred Lord Tennyson

Table of Contents

Acknowledgments

*T*hank you to every author who contributed to this book. Your stories will bring light to dark places in the hearts of many. Hope is contagious when you share it.

Peggy Willms, there are no words to express the gratitude in my heart for all that you do and the friend you are. Thank you for all you have contributed to this project.

The lighthouse is a beacon of hope for sailors lost at sea.

Thank you, Doreen Harper of Ambicionz.com for designing our beautiful cover.

But those who hope in the Lord
will renew their strength.
They will soar on wings like eagles;
they will run and not grow weary,
they will walk and not be faint.

Isaiah 40:31

FOREWORD

Stories Creating a Hopeful Tomorrow
Vincent A. Lanci

*H*ope gets us by when we expect things to work out in our favor. It can be a shining light, gravitating you toward a desired outcome, and it has for me many times. The same can be said about the opposite, and both are part of life.

In a tragic event, I learned that life combines challenging and simple moments, sunny and dark days. Despite overwhelming hopelessness, I found a *microscopic* ray of hope through hardship.

Almost a week had passed when I finally woke from a coma. While walking, I was hit by a car leaving a bar and was left for dead in the middle of the road during the middle of the night. A nurse looked at me and asked, *"Vincent, which school do you go to?"* Replying as a 21-year-old Finance student at The University of Tampa, "Pulaski Road Elementary School."

At that point in my life, "hopeless" was an understatement to describe my feelings.

I suffered a Severe Traumatic Brain Injury (TBI) and a broken tibia/fibula, resulting in a titanium rod in my leg for the rest of my life. With a brain injury, I had extreme difficulty separating dreams from reality, and the TBI was the scariest part of my journey.

I recall sitting upright in my bed, staring at a leg brace, beyond confused. I was in the hospital because of someone I'd never met, and for nothing I did wrong. I could either sit and sulk, crying, *"Why me?"* or turn the worst day of my family's life into something positive by giving hope through my story. I learned the importance of small wins, small improvements, and small gains. Minor improvements soon turned into significant accomplishments.

Present day, I have authored several mental health books for various age groups, from Toddlers to Adults. I host the podcast *A Mental Health Break* and share my story whenever possible to normalize the conversation around mental health.

I love being an entrepreneur.

Hope: as an entrepreneur, it gets you to the next day. As a Solopreneur, I have been broken down repeatedly for much of my career. Each day is filled with countless emotions. *"I am doing great!"*, *"I made a mistake."*, *"I'm on a roll!"* *"I was wrong again. I stink!"*

There are extreme highs and lows in entrepreneurship, and this journey is not for everyone, and that's okay. Some folks thrive in a 9-5 setting and make an incredible difference. After surviving the accident, I learned that 9-5 is not where I'm at my best.

In the downswings or slow periods of owning your own company, you will experience hope and hopelessness. Historically, my slowest months are from May through August, the break before the next school year.

No matter the accomplishments I experienced, I felt like I was not enough and temporarily lost hope. Then, suddenly, something shifts the momentum, a *small win* – an unexpected email with good news or unexpected money.

I am a firm believer that it only takes one. One conversation, connection, or experience can change your life forever. My childhood baseball team manager, Tom, would use this quote when we were battling adverse situations in a game. "One hit, one baserunner, or one error could change the game."

Throughout my entrepreneurial career, the most fulfilling and satisfying moments come when someone in the audience takes the time to meet me after a speaking engagement. I learn what stuck out to them, how I resonated with them, and most importantly, what I said gave them *hope*.

We are never alone on this life journey, and all have a story to share. Share yours. It may just give someone the *hope* they need.

Thank you, Teresa, for compiling these stories to create a *hopeful tomorrow*.

Hope is the foundation for creativity,
inspiration, joy and all those emotions
which allow us to transcend ourselves.

— Verena Kast in Joy,
Inspiration and Hope

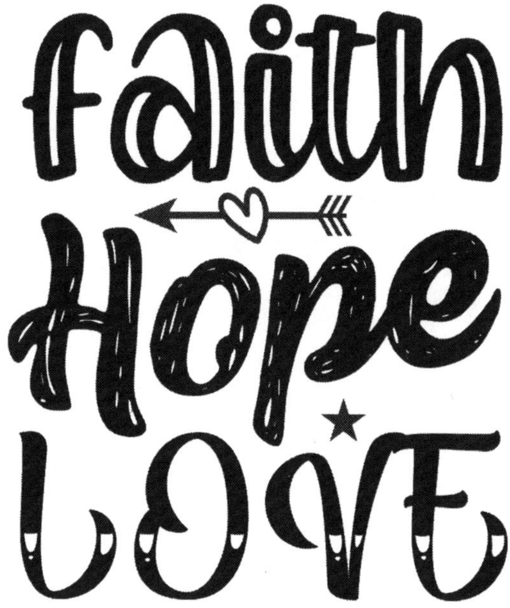
Faith
Hope
Love

Introduction

Hope is Ignited in a Grateful Heart

"*H*ope?" Many people today are asking, "What's that?"

With everything happening today, how do YOU define hope in these trying times?

Webster's dictionary says hope means: "to cherish a desire with anticipation: to want something to happen or be true." "To expect with confidence." "Trust."

The biblical definition is "To trust in, wait for, look for, or desire something or someone or to expect something beneficial in the future." (Baker's Evangelical Dictionary of Biblical Theology)

> *Now faith is confidence in what we hope for*
> *and assurance about what we do not see.* (Hebrews 11.1)

My personal belief is that faith and hope go hand in hand. My faith in God and His promises keep my hope alive. Yes, the world gives us so many reasons to lose hope. It also allows me to trust the one who created everything to bring that hope alive in me.

When I "got the God-given assignment" to create the *Daily Gift Book Series*, I dragged my feet for a long time, several years. Then, God lit a fire in my heart to collect the stories people had about Gratitude and what it meant to those who stepped up to be in that book.

A *Daily Gift of Hope* follows A *Daily Gift of Gratitude* because hope is ignited in a grateful heart. At least, that's been my experience. So here we are, holding a book filled with stories of Hope and hearts filled with Gratitude.

I hope you will experience the warmth in your heart that I have while gathering these stories.

With Great Gratitude and Many Blessings,
Teresa Velardi

The
Grateful Hearts
Community

What is the Grateful Hearts Community

O ne of the definitions in Webster's dictionary for community is:

A group linked by a common policy.

The common policy for The Grateful Hearts Community is Gratitude!

Gratitude is, according to Webster:

The state of being grateful: THANKFULNESS

Then, Webster, what is Grateful?

a: appreciative of benefits received
b: expressing gratitude

Appreciation, Gratitude, Thankfulness…. Yes, please! I'll have some of that! Why? Because grateful hearts are happier than those that aren't grateful. I like happiness, and I like abundance… yes, abundance! When we are grateful, there is always enough, even more than enough. Without gratitude, there is never enough.

It's a mindset, a perspective of how we see our lives. Whether you already have a grateful heart or want to have one, you are in the right place when you become part of The Grateful Hearts Community.

Daily inspiration, questions, quotes, scripture, and more are just a few reasons to be part of this community.

Check out our Facebook Community http://bit.ly/Grateful-Hearts

They say a person needs just three things to be truly happy in this world: someone to love, something to do, and something to hope for.

Tom Bodett

Sands of Time

by Eileen Bild

The hourglass mesmerizes.
In the passage of time
Each grain of sand slips through
To the other side.

The days of our lives
Measured by each moment.
Quietly, unstoppable.
As the ebb and flow of the ocean tide.

Descending into an eternal abyss
Offering opportunities to consider
Sands of time.
Gratitude, appreciation, grace.

As life emerges from the womb,
Fearless, bold, and empowered.
Arising in the morning sun
Reflections within the cascading waves.
A shifting of perspective.
Forever present as time seems
To be running out.
Choices made; lessons learned.
Life is the master teacher.

Hope, a path into eternity.
An outstretched hand of
The angels by our side.
Guiding with a whisper heard
Somewhere deep within.

I sit by the water's edge, focused on the pattern I am making in the sand, oblivious to what is happening around me. As a child, I could tune out the world and be immersed in my childlike wonder. The sound of the ocean lapping nearby as the slight breeze blows loose strands of hair around my face. In those precious moments lost in the passage of time, the natural evolution of growth into adulthood brings experiences filled with memories.

There is a longing to feel a sense of freedom, to explore, and really know what it's like to live. In the present, practicing daily mantras, meditations, quiet introspection, and setting intentions for tomorrow's gifts brings about hope. For a better future, the endless possibilities for change and transformation.

It is my individual responsibility to remember what it is like to look through a child's eyes, see the immense breadth of what is before me and walk my path with strength. Hope reaches beyond the veil, feels what is intangible, and gives a sense of the capability to achieve what has been deemed impossible. It is a peaceful reverie, invisible yet resting in the pulse of our hearts.

Honor your passion....
Live fearlessly....
Live the dream....

A Shred of Hope

by Jessie Tieva (Abel Isaac's Mom)

*H*ope was absent when we learned our baby's diagnosis. We were given funeral paperwork and an emotional support packet when we scheduled the c-section, but not a trace of hope. Many fake sad faces said, "I'm sorry." I was dumbfounded. It wasn't until they left with their obligatory sympathy that I burst into tears.

I was 33 weeks pregnant with my twins when I learned the baby we named Abel had trisomy 18. Google said most trisomy 18 babies die shortly after birth. I refused to believe this and searched relentlessly for stories of survivors online and on social media. Surprisingly, I found many and clung to a shred of hope.

The shred expanded as my babies were born, becoming like yarn. I wove it into a mitten as I touched Abel's tiny head, sang to him, and prayed over him while he lay in his incubator NICU bed. Days became weeks, and I rejoiced. I fought for his care every day, but providers never mentioned the future. Still, my mitten became a sweater with me and my husband weaving; others began weaving this beautiful tapestry. They, too, picked up that shred of hope and wove.

I rocked him daily when the top came off Abel's "glass" bed. I wrapped him in that shred of hope, now a blanket. His room became colorful with shreds of hope from people throughout the hospital and beyond. Abel's room illuminated colors of hope, and shreds were sticking on people's shoes as they left, weaving colors through the hospital halls, towns, and homes. A shred of hope spread far and wide.

In August, Abel's first book, featuring other children with disabilities, was published. That shred of hope became an outpouring, stretching throughout the US to countries worldwide. Parents of hundreds of children who only had a shred of hope picked up the yarn and wove their stories.

After seven incredible months, Abel passed away unexpectedly, but he touched my heart for a lifetime. The shred of hope he gave us turned into a worldwide tapestry. Hearts and minds are changed through love. Hundreds of children are now featured in his books, and the shred of hope continues.

For I know the thoughts that I think toward you,
says the Lord, thoughts of peace and not of evil,
to give you a future and a hope.

Jeremiah 29:11, NKJV

Believing HOPE

by Denise C. Herndon Harvey

*G*entle tears streamed down as thoughts again bombarded the mind. When will it ever stop? When will we find and receive the hope and peace our heart yearns for? How do you stand when all around you appears to be crumbling to pieces? How do you hold your head up and be strong for others when you only want to crawl in a ball and cry your eyes out? How often has the pain and heartache hit so hard that you can only cry out to Jesus? Yet, even in this raw state of emotions, what we see with our natural eye is subject to change.

Our hope! The hope we need, the hope we desire, and the hope that can heal our heart is found in the Lord and His Word. God's Word declares, "And not only that, but we also glory in tribulations, knowing that tribulation produces perseverance; perseverance, character; and character, hope. Now hope does not disappoint, because the love of God has been poured out in our hearts by the Holy Spirit who was given to us" (Romans 5:3-5, NKJV).

As we seek the hope we desire and put our trust in the Lord and His Word, it will not fail us. There is no going back in an attempt to change past decisions. Yet, when we allow God to operate in our hearts, those situations can and will be used for our good because God can use anything and everything to bring out a better outcome than when we began when we trust in His Word.

Seek the Lord and ask for His wisdom and understanding. Seeking the wisdom and the knowledge of His ever-present love will enable us to press on toward our predestined life purpose and remain hopeful.

H.O.P.E. (Hang. On. Pain. Ends.)

by Melanie Soloway

*T*he letters disappeared, drowned out by the unstoppable tears pouring onto the page as I wrote my plea that he not leave. Hope that the pain would dissipate didn't even enter the conversation. I was far more concerned about how I would continue to live my life without my rock and my lifeline. I did read my dad a letter I wrote while I held his hand on his deathbed; cancer had ravaged his entire body. "I'll be okay," I said softly, even though I didn't fully believe the words coming out of my mouth, "You can let go when you're ready. I love you, Dad". Watching him suffer became even more excruciating than the thought of not having him around.

When his soul exited that night, it was like watching the air around a candle flame move, transparent and visible simultaneously. The pain of his departure was worse than I imagined. Not long after he left this earth, the signs began in earnest… lyrics on the radio, pink heart-shaped clouds in the sky. I dismissed them as illusions of a desperate daughter trying to hold onto her daddy. Then, a butterfly appeared while I was hiking, and I knew he was there, letting me know he hadn't left me. More signs came as time marched on, and so did the healing.

Many say time heals all wounds or things will improve over time. I've learned during the 24 years since my dad left this earth that it's not time that heals but what I do with the time when difficulties occur. The key to healing is tapping into the trinity of connection and strengthening all three parts: connection to self, source, and others, bringing the past, present, and future into alignment, and me into alignment with myself, my soul, and my source. Trusting the path, process, and signs creates harmony in my mind, body, and spirit. When we shift our focus, hope can re-emerge. When we take necessary action, allow the feelings to come up, and let the tears out, pain washes away, and hope returns with joy and happiness again.

In fact, hope is best gained
after defeat and failure,
because then inner strength
and toughness is produced.

Fritz Knapp

Daily Dose Of Hope

by Jacki Long

*H*aving grown up singing and playing the piano, I learned at a young age what music can do for one's soul. I learned about love, friendship, resilience, determination, and loads of fun. I also learned that when life is hard, music soothes and provides hope.

Recently, I had the pleasure of attending the symphony. In the past, it wasn't my choice of music as vocals are often absent. Lyrics were typically more important to me than instrumentals. However, on this occasion, it was different.

During the cacophony of the orchestra, I heard the rise and fall of emotion; the sadness turned into great joy and revelation. Of what is to come. Of what lies ahead. Celebration in the lessons learned, especially lessons the most painful experiences bring.

Since the betrayal and ultimate loss of lifelong friends and people I trusted for most of my life, grief, and sadness have been part of my daily life. I don't mourn all the time. It's like a dark cloud that sometimes shows up yet wearily goes away.

I actively seek lessons I am to learn from their betrayal. I'm choosing a better life. I'm choosing better relationships, those where loyalty, honesty, and integrity are reciprocated.

The emotion I felt during the symphony was unexpected and welcomed. A welcome reminder that life has ups and downs. When there are downs, I can remember that the black cloud shows itself temporarily and that sunnier days ahead are promised and more frequent.

HAVE patience and never LOSE HOPE

A Dragonfly Gave Me Hope
by Katerina Pappas

*H*ope is a funny thing. Unlike kindness or optimism, it cannot be achieved directly. To truly feel hope, something inside must radically shift. From my experience, moments of profound inner shift are unplanned and come from beyond our conscious efforts.

They result from an unseen connection with something beyond ourselves. One could say moments with God. My moments with God tend to unfold through nature and animals.

For a couple of years, I've struggled with relationships. Friendships I'd nurtured most of my life were crumbling and slipping through my fingers. While I saw the red flags, my efforts to find mutual understanding were hitting a wall. I felt powerless and at a loss.

During this hard and lonely time, a certain winged messenger came along. On a Wednesday morning, upon opening my front door to go for my morning walk, I heard a loud buzzing sound. I looked around but couldn't tell where it was coming from… until something told me to look up.

There she was, a gorgeous, quite humongous dragonfly that had somehow flown into the halls of my outdoor second-floor condo. For some reason, instead of flying out the way she came in, she insisted on trying to get through a small glass window on the ceiling! How could she not know the way to freedom was all around her or that she was fighting a losing battle?

Part of me deeply resonated with her struggle. It was excruciating to watch her fling her body on the windowpane repeatedly. I also felt stuck in loops of failed attempts to connect with people I once loved.

The next morning, she was still stuck. I felt terrible and went out with a broom to guide her away from the window, but it only made her cling to her spot more. That, too, felt very familiar.

That night, I prayed to God to help me relinquish control over the fate of this creature. Without realizing it, what I prayed for was hope. Hope that she would fly into the clear, that she could set herself free, and that I could set myself free.

I delayed leaving the next morning, fearing she would still be stuck. But when I opened the door and looked up, she was gone. My prayer was answered.

Let your hopes, not your hurts,
shape your future.

Robert H. Schuller

Never Walk Alone

by Sonia Waite

I've often wondered, "Is this really my life?"

It seemed so long ago that I was confident and excited for each new day.

I enjoyed my family life, had great relationships with wonderful friends, and cultivated meaningful connections within my community. I thought I had it all! A job I loved, a great husband, fantastic children, relatively good health, and a firm belief in God as my source, friend, and stay. Then, everything slowly fell apart when the career I loved for multiple decades ended. I felt hopeless and lost. But God, through His word, reminded me of His promises, "And the Lord is the One who goes ahead of you; He will be with you. He will not fail you or forsake you. Do not fear or be dismayed." Deuteronomy 31:8

Although I knew God's promises, anxiety, and fear for my new normal caused me great dis-ease. Again, God reminded me, "Have I not commanded you? Be strong and courageous! Do not tremble or be dismayed, for the Lord your God is with you wherever you go." Joshua 1:9

When new opportunities I earnestly prayed for didn't appear, I again felt hopeless. Like before, through His word, my God reminded me of His promise: "And my God shall supply all your needs according to His riches in glory in Christ Jesus." Philippians 4:19

After years of waiting, the opportunity to start my own business became a reality. As I move forward, I take comfort in knowing, "I can do all things through Him who strengthens me." Philippians 4:13

Today, I continue to grow in all areas, knowing the Lord my God is with me, and His word comforts me, "Yet those who wait for the Lord will gain new strength; they will mount up with wings like eagles, they will run and not get tired, they will walk and not become weary." Isaiah 40:31

If feeling hopeless, allow God's truth to anchor your heart, mind, and soul: "Wait for the Lord; Be strong, and let your heart take courage; Yes, wait for the Lord." Psalms 27:14

Hope Is a Choice

by Mark O'Brien

I don't know if this is true for anyone else. But for me, parenting was a matter of common sense. Except in cases of obvious and serious injury or illness, I felt pretty well equipped to do what needed to be done in most circumstances. If my sons were hungry, I fed them. If they were hurt, physically or emotionally, I comforted them. If they were undertaking something positive, I supported and encouraged them. If they were undertaking something less positive, I discouraged them and explained why I was doing so. If they got into trouble, I stood by them while they endured the consequences earned by the trouble they'd caused or gotten into.

Along the way, I somehow had the wherewithal to tell them there are just two fundamental motivations in the world. Those motivations are fear and hope. I shared my conviction that people who were motivated by hope — presuming they weren't deliberately stupid or blindly naïve — had far less to fear than those who were motivated by it. I suggested if they believed they could do something — or wanted to achieve something passionately enough — they likely would. And I suggested if they believed they couldn't do something, they'd be self-fulfilling right.

By teaching my sons those things, I also learned some very valuable lessons. I learned if you raise your children with the hopefulness you espouse, that hopefulness will be consistently contagious. If you stand by your children and make it evident, you'll always be there and never quit on them. They'll be comforted by knowing where the lines are (just as the startle reflexes of infants are comforted by their swaddling blankets), even as they confidently and constructively explore the world beyond those lines in their own ways, at their own paces.

I don't know if this is true for anyone else. But the more hopeful I am, the lighter I find in the world. The more hopeful I am, the fewer things I fear. The older I get, the surer I am that hope is the right choice.

*All kids need is a little help, a little hope
and somebody who believes in them.*

Magic Johnson

Hope

by Robyn M. Drothler

*P*arents come to me looking for HOPE. They are looking for anything they can do to help their child who is struggling. I become the catalyst for that mission. As a professional in the field of speech pathology, I am able to provide insight and strategies to achieve that goal.

My favorite part of the job helping kids learn to talk is when they really start making the connections to communicate and initiate talking, which brings out their personalities. I love it when what was previously gibberish is now "clear-enough" communication and verbalizations to know what they have been trying to say all along! This newly formed connection brings on a newfound confidence with kids, which is amazing to watch!

Many times, mispronouncing words is what prevents a child from being understood despite having the vocabulary and knowing the right words to say. It is my job to help parents help their kids connect meaning for them to express themselves clearly. It is through this process that the parents gain HOPE. They finally see the light at the end of the tunnel that was previously too difficult to navigate on their own. They finally see the possibilities of engaging with their children in new ways, new conversations emerge, and they see a brighter future for their children.

All too often, a family will come to me and say the last therapist they were with said their child would never talk. Without having the ability to see in the future, there is no way a therapist could say that with confidence. It is with the tools and strategies, and commitment to making a difference that progress is made. What once were baby steps slowly become giant steps, and then the child learns to communicate and speak on their own. HOPE is formed.

Finding Love Again After 80!

It is never too late to rejuvenate.

by Brooke Peterson

*L*ife changes, and in November of 2020, the news was truly an upset. My husband, Bob Peterson's diagnosis from the Veteran's Administration head of the Renal division threw a monkey wrench into our life plans. The phone call to tell me that his renal disease had morphed into 'fatal' and 'End Stage Renal Failure' was imminent.

His disease progressed, but he did not leave the planet for nine more months. His family was with him weekly and stayed as he passed. We 'pampered' him and let him have anything he wanted to eat or drink. No restrictions now! The doctor said it would be worse on me and brought in Hospice.

What now? There was no insurance, but the Veterans handled many of the charges.

I was now alone, and after 41 years of his companionship, I desired and hoped for more.

I decided to go on the internet. Within weeks, I had multiple reachouts to my handle of 'I love to cook.'

My search quickly landed on another 'Bob' who was a mountain man. He had been a NEIGHBOR more than forty years prior. But we had never met.

In September, we met halfway and had an instant connection.

Our meeting was the first of many! After taking a 30-day trip across the US on a train the following September, we decided we liked being together! We use our middle names, and Bryn and Brooke became a couple.

November 2022 was when I moved into his Santa Cruz Mountain home. We have both integrated beautifully and fallen deeper in love. He was 82 in April, and I was 81 in May!

Neither of us ever thought we could find both companionship and love again. Good News! You can!

All the great things are simple, and many
can be expressed in a single word
freedom, justice, honor, duty, mercy, hope.

Winston Churchill

We Don't Know
What We Don't Know

by Peggy Willms

I am an optimistic realist. Give me the data, and we will find a positive solution. Most everyone has been in a situation where they have felt out of control, outside their comfort zone, or trapped. For me, not having answers checks off all of the above.

Some people would rather not know a medical diagnosis and have the motto, "We are all going to die sometime, somehow." Me? I will do anything within my power to determine "what is wrong" so I can find solutions to improve it. Why am I tired? Why did I gain 17 pounds in one month? Why have I had pneumonia six times and more sinus infections than letters in the alphabet? Why is my brain foggy? Why? Why? I felt like a toddler seeking answers.

Answers give hope, and I have no family history to compare against. I have never met my paternal father, and my mother never went to the doctor until she had Multiple Sclerosis and passed away in 2021. So I chose to give my sons my history: hypothyroidism, Hashimoto's, IGA Deficiency, osteoporosis, anxiety, OCD, chronic neutropenia, hiatal hernia…shall I go on? Once I had answers to my "what," I could put my big girl panties on and find healthier solutions to either live with or improve some of these conditions. Many times the medical world or even family and friends struggle to understand you don't feel well, especially when many issues are not visible.

I pressed on for years, thinking I was spinning too many plates to feel good. Busy people don't feel great, right? I didn't sleep or eat well. But my intuition (and personality) do not take no for an answer. Once blood results validated my symptoms, I could fine-tune medication and my lifestyle and began living again. Hope helps you press on, and when you move even one inch at a time, eventually, your hope becomes reality.

A Caribbean Beacon in Brooklyn

by Rhonda Douglas Charles

*I*n the hustle and bustle of New York's high-end society, Marjorie, a first-generation immigrant from the Caribbean, wore her role as a nanny with grace and pride. Each morning, she would arrive at a grand brownstone, her every step echoing stories of sunlit beaches and warm island breezes as she cared for the children of a prominent family.

Yet, beneath the veneer of her daily duties, Marjorie harbored dreams that soared higher than the skyscrapers. Once the children left for school, Marjorie exchanged her nanny hat for books every day, diving into her studies at Brooklyn College. The subway rides were her quiet reflection time, where dreams of her past and ambitions for the future intertwined.

Her dedication wasn't without challenges. Balancing her responsibilities and education demanded sacrifices and sleepless nights. But Marjorie's resilience, a gift from her Caribbean roots, and the encouragement from the family she served saw her through. The children, noticing her unwavering commitment, often asked, "Marjorie, why do you study so hard?" With a warm smile, she'd reply, "So I can teach children like you to reach for the stars, no matter where they come from."

Years passed, and with them came the proud day Marjorie became a U.S. citizen. Her journey didn't stop there. Marjorie's hard work culminated in her becoming a special education teacher with the NYC Board of Ed. She now stood in front of a classroom, shaping young minds, including those of fellow immigrants, teaching them that there's always hope, always an opportunity to rise.

Marjorie's story serves as a beacon of hope, illuminating the path for countless immigrants who come to the U.S. seeking a brighter future. It's a testament that survival jobs are but stepping stones, and with determination and belief, anyone can transition from merely surviving to truly thriving.

Marjorie's life whispers a message to all immigrants: "Your dreams are valid. Let them fly, for the sky is not the limit but just the beginning.

Hope is being able to see that there is light despite all of the darkness.

Desmond Tutu

Hope To Live Again

by Maxine Tomlinson

*L*ord, can I please wake up from this dream?

This is not how it was supposed to be! All our dreams and plans could not end here. Could they?

We had taken such a leap of faith and returned home to raise a farm and live off the land. We knew it would not be easy, but we were young, strong, resilient, and full of ideas.

We were certain we had heard from God. We knew that the family's obstacles would be an issue, but we felt certain they would come around to wanting the family plantation to be vibrant and prosperous again. Unfortunately, they fought us at every turn. They lacked the vision and did not want to let go of control out of fear.

Peter had agonized over it and had made himself sick. His relationship with his dad had deteriorated even more, although there was not much there to begin with. His dad abandoned him and his mother at age one and did not keep commitments over the next 32 years.

Sitting here watching the children playing around the grave site was almost surreal. Rachel was nine years, Deborah seven, and Simon. Did they grasp the enormity of the situation? Their father was in the ground, and we were on our own, and I didn't have a clue what to do from here! They had such a peace and calm about them; it could only be God.

I drew strength from that. I knew that if I could continue to make them happy and not traumatized, we could survive. They had to be my focus going forward. It was as if God was saying… trust Me, follow Me closely, and I will work out for good what seems to be so insurmountable and devastating right now.

NEVER lose hope

A Surrogate's Journey

by Alysia Lyons

*A*t sixteen, I decided that I never wanted to have children, but I always knew I wanted to experience pregnancy. I offered to have a baby for someone long before I actually knew that was possible. Ten years later, falling in love and a biological clock changed my mind about having a baby of my own, and once my mind changed, I wanted that baby *yesterday*! Ultimately, it took 18 months to get pregnant. I could not describe a purer form of torture for an impatient person.

A year and a half later, I was given the opportunity to become a surrogate. When I met the first couple I carried a baby for, their story shocked me. They'd been waiting 30 years to have their baby. The second woman I had a baby for was opting to be a single mom because she had never found the right partner. My next surrogacy journey was with a couple who had found a second chance at love later in life. My final journey was for another single mom. She tried carrying a baby herself but miscarried at nine weeks. A friend of hers said, "That soul will come back to you." They transferred one embryo, and six weeks later, during our heartbeat check, the doctor found two heartbeats. Two identical girls were born nine months later.

For 18 months, my struggle taught me compassion for women who desperately wanted a child and couldn't have one on their own. Being a mother has been the greatest joy in my life, and it has been my privilege to bring six children into this world, even though only one of those was mine to keep.

Hope is like a road in the country;
there was never a road, but when many people
walk on it, the road comes into existence.

Lin Yutang

164 Times

by Faith James

*H*OPE is mentioned 164 times in the Bible! That is how important and necessary it is to our daily lives.

So, how do you activate HOPE? You must first activate faith. Having faith leads to hope.

Faith is not just my name; it's my operating system for my personal life and business. I identify as the Daughter of Abraham and Child of The King!

One spiritual concept that I have leaned on and that served me well to operate in hope, no matter the external circumstances confidently, is that *God and I are a majority.* I know I will run and finish my race well with God on my side.

"For I know the plans I have for you, declares the Lord, plans to prosper you and not to harm you, plans to give you hope and a future. Matthew 19:26 But Jesus looked at them and said, 'With man this is impossible, but with God all things are possible." - Jeremiah 29:11

God is not a liar. His word is truth. And so, my hope is anchored in Him.

Here are some ways I stay anchored in hope, and my wish is that these serve you well.

- **Read The Bible Daily:** Develop a practice of reading your Bible daily. Start with Psalm 23, Psalm 91, and Colossians 1:9-14

- **Journal Your Gratitude to God Daily:** Start each entry this way, "I am so happy and grateful to God now that all is well with me, and I am vibrationally and divinely aligned to health, wealth, and abundance.

This practice of daily scripture and gratitude journaling is something my clients do, and they have seen great results. My wish is that this practice does the same for you.

Faith without works is dead.

James 2:26

Psalm 91

¹ Whoever dwells in the shelter of the Most High will rest in the shadow of the Almighty.[a]

² I will say of the Lord, "He is my refuge and my fortress, my God, in whom I trust."

³ Surely he will save you from the fowler's snare and from the deadly pestilence.

⁴ He will cover you with his feathers, and under his wings you will find refuge; his faithfulness will be your shield and rampart.

⁵ You will not fear the terror of night, nor the arrow that flies by day,

⁶ nor the pestilence that stalks in the darkness, nor the plague that destroys at midday.

⁷ A thousand may fall at your side, ten thousand at your right hand, but it will not come near you.

⁸ You will only observe with your eyes and see the punishment of the wicked.

⁹ If you say, "The Lord is my refuge," and you make the Most High your dwelling,

¹⁰ no harm will overtake you, no disaster will come near your tent.

¹¹ For he will command his angels concerning you to guard you in all your ways;

¹² they will lift you up in their hands, so that you will not strike your foot against a stone.

¹³ You will tread on the lion and the cobra; you will trample the great lion and the serpent.

¹⁴ "Because he loves me," says the Lord, "I will rescue him; I will protect him, for he acknowledges my name.

¹⁵ He will call on me, and I will answer him; I will be with him in trouble, I will deliver him and honor him.

¹⁶ With long life I will satisfy him and show him my salvation."

Survivorcate

by Dr. Beth Goodman, aka Dr. Sprinkles

*M*y life is a testament to faith, hope, and the incredible strength of the human spirit. I am a 16-year breast cancer surTHRIVER, standing as a beacon of hope for others navigating this challenging journey. Through my experiences, I embrace the profound wisdom of Psalm 118:17, "I shall not die, but live, and declare the works of the Lord," and the guidance in Proverbs 3:5-6, "Trust in the Lord with all your heart and lean not on your own understanding; in all your ways submit to him, and he will make your paths straight."

My journey began in 11th grade with a benign lumpectomy on my right breast. Lumpectomies on my left breast in 2000, 2002, and 2004 were also benign. Then, in 2007, the lumpectomy results were malignant. "Ms. Goodman, you have Ductal Carcinoma In Situ...DCIS."

I responded, "What is THAT, and is it on sale?"

"You have breast cancer."

"I will live and not die!" The diagnosis shook my very foundation, yet my faith unwavered. Fear was never allowed in. I trusted God, believing there was a purpose and all things worked together, even this! Armed with faith and pink praise pumps, I embarked on a rigorous treatment plan, determined to conquer the disease. I had cancer. Cancer did not have me.

Through surgery and treatments, I leaned on Proverbs 3:5-6 as a guiding light, trusting that God's plan was unfolding even when I couldn't see it. Unwavering trust carried me through, enabling me to "sprinkle" others with hope and faith.

I'm called to be a Survivorcate... an advocate for Survivors to LIVE OUT LOUD! Through my survivor's journey and the stories of those I've met, I understand that cancer does not define us. Instead, it reveals the strength within us and the power of community. My life's mission is to sprinkle hope into those who walk this path, reminding them that even in the face of adversity, there is light, and in moments of doubt, faith will carry us forward.

I have witnessed the incredible resilience of the human spirit to rise above adversity. With faith as our compass and the support of a loving community, we can navigate the stormy seas of cancer, emerging as "Sprinklers" of hope for one another and the world.

God had given me hope! Darkness comes.
In the middle of it, the future looks blank.
The temptation to quit is huge. Don't.
You are in good company...
You will argue with yourself that there is
no way forward.
But with God, nothing is impossible.
He has more ropes and ladders and tunnels
out of pits than you can conceive.
Wait. Pray without ceasing. Hope.

John Piper

Hope Does Not Disappoint

by Pastor Jack Rehill

*R*om. 5:5 says, "Now hope does not disappoint, because the love of God has been poured out in our hearts by the Holy Spirit."

Hope is rooted in love, the love that God has for us that moved Him to give us His only begotten Son, that whoever believes in Him would not perish but have everlasting life. This is the ultimate hope, and it will not disappoint us.

How many of us have suffered disappointment in this life, in this world? We had hoped that our marriage would be forever, only to find out that our husband or wife had taken up with another. We had hoped for the job of our dreams, only to find out we couldn't make the grade. We had hoped that our loved one would be healed, only to find out that they did not survive.

Such was the case with Martha and Mary and their brother Lazarus in John 11. They had hoped that Jesus would come and heal him, but He stayed two more days where He was, and their brother died. Where was He?

But that wasn't the end of the story. Jesus, the resurrection, and the life, raised him from the dead to demonstrate the ultimate hope we have to live on daily. Whatever disappointment we have suffered in this life, we will never suffer in the life to come.

It is Christ in us, His character formed in us, that gives us the hope of the glory to come, and it will come. It is a hope we can count on every day, above and beyond whatever the day may bring.

The apostle Paul said, "I know whom I have believed, and am per-suaded that He is able to keep what I have committed to Him until that day."

FIND JOY IN THE Journey

Negative Programs

by Dr. Markus Wettstein

*M*y hope is to find freedom from as many negative programs as possible not only at me but also at all humanity.

Negative programs are apps placed in our subconscious. When it comes to learned behavior, we can already see negativity creeping in. Addictions are extremely negative learned behaviors.

Some programs are learned and groomed over the years. "You can't have fun if you don't drink alcohol." But even small programs, like cutting into traffic, are worth looking into. It takes me a while to stop the adrenaline from triggering negative thoughts, even if I was the one cut off. Driving aggressively isn't necessary, and I now leave enough space for cutters. As a result, arriving at work or home is set by a different tone. As a result, I enjoy my job more and likely make better decisions.

The most significant change in my life was changing my attitude towards money. As outlined in my story in the first book of the *All Things Wellness* book series, money equaled survival for my post-war parents. Therefore, they taught their children that money was the end all, be all. For me, that program did not lead to happiness. Yes, earning reasonable amounts of money relieves some of the pressure, but then the wants take over the needs. Targeted advertisement is very good at reaching our subconscious. We buy stuff we do not need! We accumulate credit card debt—a beginning to our enslavement. Suddenly, we HAVE to work to pay back the debt. Taking any job just to get the money is a recipe for dissatisfaction. This feeds negative feelings that only serve to keep us in a negative thought space. So, I do not carry credit card debt. I only keep a small loan for my car to keep up my credit score. This is obviously an oxymoron, as your credit score is meaningless if you do not have credit; another program highly valued in our society that is relatively meaningless to me.

Negative programs are easy to spot; they do not lead to a positive life. We are so busy these days it takes extra effort to analyze our own behavior. Join me on the path to positivity.

You are full of unshaped dreams…
You are laden with beginnings…
There is hope in you…

Lola Ridge

Hope in Nature

by Melody Dixon

Simone gets up at the crack of dawn, ready to efficiently tackle the "To-Do-List of the Day."

On this morning, she was more introspective than gung-ho. Something was off, and she could not put her finger on it. All she knew was that today could not be the same old, same old.

She pondered her life. In retrospect, she thought she was living but realized she was not. Not in the true sense of the word. "Everything was getting taken care of, right?', she thought. The kids, the home life, and her business. With a jolt, she realized she was nowhere on this list of things to take care of.

She heard a voice say, "Go take a walk in the backyard and clear your head." She obeyed. She entered the dark laundry room and turned the knob of the door that led to the backyard. The most glorious sunshine flooded the room, blinding her for an instant. She paused as her eyes adjusted, then stepped onto the soft, dew-drenched grass from the back porch.

The voice said, "Look around you. Look at the birds of the air, for they neither sow nor reap nor gather into barns; yet your heavenly Father feeds them. Are you not of more value than they?" Simone, the act of always doing says you don't trust God to do what he says he will do. She felt chastened and closed her eyes. The voice continued, "I know where that way of being comes from, but you have got to let it go and BE outdoors and watch me take care of you. Your life will be as good as you allow it to be."

The next morning, as soon as she was dressed, she bounded into the backyard and frolicked around in gratitude. Noticing the birds, flowers, and, most importantly, the joy and peace in her heart as she knew she was taken care of.

Story of Hope

by Shantay Adams

*G*od is indeed the God of hope, and He gives hope to the hopeless, Lamentation 3:24 (AMP).

Recently, I published a book called "Release the Honey Within You: Seven Keys to Beautify the Overly Aggressive to Become a Virtue Honeybee." One day, while visiting various venues to host the book launch, I met a lady named Paula. She operates a recreational center. We discussed the book and her marriage as she gave me a tour. Paula confided to me the state of her marriage, which needed healing and restoration, but she was at a point of hopelessness.

As I began sharing strategies and tools with her, I learned Paula was open to receiving. I could see her countenance beginning to change in our hour-or-so conversation outside in the sun. She shared she knew this was a God moment because, privately, she had been praying to the Lord for guidance concerning her marriage. She realized the Lord heard her cry and spoke through me to encourage her, give her hope, wisdom, and guidance.

Her marriage of nearly three decades had become dry and unhealthy, but it was her set time of favor to be watered for healing, health, and restoration in her marriage. In addition, the more Paula and I spoke about honey, the more the atmosphere around us became sweeter! I told her the more she releases honey, the more her atmosphere at home will shift in her favor. I gave her a free copy of the book based on the conversation. A few days later, I stopped by to check on her, and she stated, "I had a come to a Jesus moment reading your book." She went on to say, "I took the advice given, and I am ready to do the work for a healthy marriage."

You will face many defeats in your life,
but never let yourself be defeated.

Maya Angelou

The Department of Hope

by Tammy Hader

*H*ope doesn't come easy to a realist like me. Neither does luck. I tend to make my opportunities rather than have them appear as if magic or miracles are afoot. Hope feels a little like part of a saintly job description way above my pay grade. The best I can do is ask the heavenly staff to grant my desire for all things good and happy. Whether my request is granted or not, the clock keeps ticking, and I move forward in my life.

Today is a good day, filled with accomplishments. Mom's hair is cut, her refrigerator freezer is stocked with frozen meals, and her car is fueled up and ready for short trips to the pharmacy, Taco Bell, and her friend Barbara's home. She keeps on going amid the typical aches and pains of an 83-year-old. She insisted on buying a couple of lottery tickets while we were at the gas station. She enjoys occasionally crossing her fingers for a miracle sequence of numbers. The smile on her face is worth a lot more than the two-dollar pieces of paper now resting on my kitchen island.

After returning home, I enjoy the warmth caressing my cheeks during my afternoon walk to the mailbox. I am not alone on this good day. Neighbors emerge from their winter fortresses to bask in the invisible promise of springtime floating on the breeze. Standing at the mailboxes, we chat about the weather, our cats, and last month's neighborhood bunko game—no need to rush back to the shelter to escape bitter winter windchills. The grass is beginning to turn green again, and trees are starting to bud.

Walking back home, each street I pass contains my people. They smile, wave, and yell out a greeting, "Hi, Tammy!" The employees in the celestial department of hope are working overtime in my neighborhood this afternoon. Mom's lottery tickets did not win, but a magic beyond luck was afoot in the warmth of sunshine, a neighbor's wave, and a mother's smile.

ENJOY THE
simple
THINGS

Dogs Being Dogs

by Jodie Fitzgerald

When I was a child, about six years old, I remember a cute puppy that was a few months old. I remember walking down my street with this puppy, probably dancing and singing to him.

The next thing I remember, I was on the ground, with the puppy holding and tugging on the scarf around my neck. Both my hands were holding the tight scarf so that I could breathe. Every time I wiggled or tried anything to get the puppy to let go, the puppy pulled harder. He played happily, thinking it was a game. Finally, a lady came with a broom and got the puppy to let go.

I've always remembered this experience; although it was a dangerous situation, the puppy was playing. The puppy did not seem aggressive. He thought this was a fun game.

When dogs become pets, I believe they are misunderstood, and their genetic needs and instincts are forgotten. This puppy was playing out a genetic trait, and my yelling and squirming probably made it more fun for the pup.

This is just one example of how fast and easily a puppy can be misunderstood. Stepping into the dog's paws really taking over what the dog is experiencing and going through is vital and important for every dog.

We have put these animals into our lives with high expectations that they will fit easily into our homes and lives. That is why I have created The Paws & Hearts Club with the hope of providing information about the dogs' truth, create clarity, and find solutions to build amazing relationships that last a lifetime.

So that dogs can be dogs.

Hope is the thing with feathers that perches
in the soul and sings the tune
without the words and never stops at all.

Emily Dickinson

Hope Inspires

by Johnny Tan

*T*he first time the word "Hope" truly registered in my mind as an impactful aspiration was when my mom assured me that I would somehow make it to the United States to attend college after I graduated high school at 17 years old in Melaka, Malaysia. Growing up, I was always on the lookout for – "Hoping" that all the bells and whistles of life would fall right into my lap, as some would call it, wishful thinking!

It wasn't until I was a freshman at Louisiana State University, four months after my 18th birthday halfway around the world, that the word "Hope" finally sank into my consciousness as the unique feeling of expectation and desire was real and did happen. Since then, the word seems to be my guiding flashlight whenever I need assistance to achieve a goal that may initially look unattainable.

After my dad's sudden passing in my sophomore year, «Hope" was all I had to inspire me to continue with my life's plan of being in the U.S. It led me to meet eight incredible women who became my surrogate moms. Collectively, my nine Moms constantly reminded me of the power of "Hope" while I was pursuing my life's dreams and desires, as it had contributed to their successes. They are right! I recall many a time, just when I thought I was out for the count, I was able to muster the strength and courage to push forward, as each day "Hope" provided me with a fresh, clean sheet of paper to start over - create, plan, act, and not give up!

Over the years, I have experienced plenty of unexpected tearful setbacks; however, the unwavering power of "Hope" inspires me every morning, leading to eventual successful rebounds and arriving at my highest self!

Gift of Hope

by Lucia Murphy

I have found true love.

In 2013, I began going to my dad's gravesite daily when my ex-husband was busy at work. I would sit there anywhere from half an hour to a full hour, asking for a better life. I wasn't happy in my marriage at all.

My ex-husband and I were really nothing more than friends and should never have gotten married. Our marriage was extremely toxic. There was a lot of verbal abuse by him and his parents, never physical, but I had simply had enough.

In 2014, I threw myself a 40th birthday party because I never had friends growing up. I was always the black sheep in kindergarten, grade school, high school, and college. True friends know who they are, but they were very small and in between.

A gentleman had walked in and asked if I knew who he was. I didn't at the time until he showed me a picture of his former self vs. his new self. I immediately threw my arms around him and exclaimed, "You are the best birthday present I've ever received from God and my dad! "I knew that my prayers had been answered.

In 2015, I needed someone to go to a wedding with because my ex-husband wouldn't support a gay wedding, so I asked this gentleman who came to my party in November if he wanted to be my date. I immediately told my ex-husband, "I can't control what's going to happen next." The wedding was wonderful. We had an astonishing time. Within five months, I moved out, moved on, and I started dating this wonderful man.

I became his wife on 10/03/2020.

I love you, Glynn. Thank you, Dad, and thank you, God, for listening to my prayers.

PS: On 10-26-2022, I gave everything to God 100%, and I am closer than ever before.

Hope is not an emotion;
it's a way of thinking or a cognitive process.

Brené Brown

Inspiring Story of Resilience

by Martariesa Logue

I was born with Thrombocytopenia-Absent Radius (TAR) syndrome, marked by the absence of a bone called the radius in each forearm and a shortage of blood cells involved in platelets — a condition I now proudly embrace.

My parents' unshakable determination led them to choose parenthood, defying counsel to consider abortion due to my limb difference. Their courage became my anchor in the face of adversity and a physician's prognosis of intellectual limitations. I stand today as living proof that such claims are mere fallacies.

Remarkably, my wrists have never required surgical intervention. While I grappled with splints and battled low platelet counts, I persevered and adapted. My parents fostered an environment of determination devoid of pity. In educational institutions, nurturing teachers facilitated my journey toward normalcy. They adapted tools and supported my growth. Despite financial constraints, my parents encouraged exploration, partnering with organizations like the Shriners to ensure my potential remained limitless. From baby beauty pageants to gymnastics, my formative years were rich with diverse experiences. High school witnessed my multifaceted engagement in sports, music, and leadership roles. Academically thriving, I led clubs and represented my peers. My pursuit of education led to a business-focused associate degree before venturing into paralegal studies at the bachelor's level.

Today, as the Assistant Director for the Virtual Learning Academy, I contribute to fostering a digital learning environment. My commitment to the community is evident through volunteering at a local Community Center and the church's Tech Team. Challenges, though inevitable, have been met with unwavering fortitude. My parents and I chose a path that celebrated my innate self—untouched by surgical alteration, my absence of radius bones tells a unique and powerful story. Let my journey be a beacon of hope. Embrace your uniqueness, for it is your strength. Overcoming challenges reveals your true potential.

Ask To See

by Andrew M Foster

When I pray, I pray for prayer
to express words that play on
endless dishonest endeavors.

Before I sink my knees into the floor,
I reflect on paths that guide me to
wooded places, jungles where steps and

ladders arise out of life's image.
At dawn, the sun remains between
the horizon, clouds speak its light

though I hold onto the night:
something not seen grooved with
shades not from trees.

When I spread my hands out, I reach
for staffs that relieve burdens yet
the world is weighing down on my shoulders.

When I pray, I pray for prayer
in hope of seeing how the Creator sees
without penny-pinching flaws, just
to add a quarter to my vision.

Hope never abandons you, you abandon it.

George Weinberg

Kindness Inspires Joy

by Bonita Joy

I stood, waiting for the stoplight to turn green, when I heard my name called. I turned and saw a man named Joseph who said, "You probably don't recognize me, but you made a significant impact on my life."

"I did?" I exclaimed.

Joseph explained that three years earlier, he had phoned me from Northern California after he lost his home in a wildfire. He was confused and in shock and didn't know where to go.

He had called me in response to an online rental ad for a house I managed, as he had a distant connection to the town. Joseph said I was so encouraging on the phone about finding an affordable home for rent that he decided to make the two-thousand-mile journey to Lawrence, Kansas.

I showed him a home when he arrived. That home didn't work out, but he felt "welcomed and invited by me." Unbeknownst to me, Joseph relocated to Lawrence and wanted to thank me face-to-face for inspiring him to take the risk and make the journey. "Thank you," he said, "for being who you are, all the work you do, and being as kind and friendly as you are."

Joseph referenced my middle name, "Joy," He explained that when he was in a dark, sad, and grieving place, meeting me was part of opening up to a joyful life and a joyful experience. He expressed heartfelt gratitude, complete with his hands upon his heart.

This reunion made my day. It also helped me realize that we may inspire hope for others while simply going about our daily lives. We don't always know when someone is in a dark place. In a time of division in the world, we may unknowingly have a huge impact with a seemingly small act of kindness.

Imagine the impact if we CONSCIOUSLY encouraged hope. Regardless of the circumstances, let's be kind and inspire everyday moments of JOY for others.

Familiar Windows

by Chris Crouse

*T*he morning light poured into the room through familiar windows. I rose from a troubled slumber, got out of bed, walked over to the window, and stared. My home. At least it was. At that moment, an overwhelming flood of emotions swept me under the current of rejection. I felt betrayed, despised, unloved, and unwanted. I was fourteen and was stripped of my mother's care.

I remember crying and questioning everything. Then I heard the sweetest voice on the planet ask, "Chris, would you like some breakfast?" It was my grandmother. She was a truly precious woman, full of wisdom and love. I wiped a few tears away and said yes. I told her that I would be there momentarily. I needed to run some water over my face to not give away that I was shedding tears. Somehow, she knew anyway.

Looking back on that morning, I realize that the sad emotions tied to rejection were not worth all the energy that it absorbed from me. My mother was a troubled soul and took her pain out on us children. That is why I was removed from her care and the home that I lived in for almost 14 years. Now, at 57 years old, I look back and thank God for that morning. That morning, the sun brought new life to my heart. I felt alive for the very first time. No more hateful screams of utter disappointment from my mother's voice that constantly filled my youthful ears. No more battle wounds from my mother's hand. The war against me was over. My world was safe.

My uncle became like an older brother, and my grandmother and grandfather were just that, a mother and father of the grandest kind. I am so grateful for that morning because God answered my prayers for a better life.

*Everything that is done
in the world is done by hope.*

Martin Luther

Hope Springs Eternal

by Alan Jude Summa

"*H*ope springs eternal." What does that even mean? To understand its meaning, we must first define "Hope." According to the dictionary, Hope is *a desire accompanied by expectation of, or belief in fulfillment.* So "Hope springs eternal" can be defined as *The feeling of hopefulness endlessly renewing itself,* or *It is human nature always to find fresh cause for optimism.*

This means that it is in our nature to Hope. Our Creator has hardwired into our DNA to expect good things and to believe in the probability of a positive outcome, despite how devastating or dire our circumstances are. Therefore, since Hope is indeed instilled in us by our Creator, our Creator will always be part of shaping the outcome.

Hope can be fulfilled by a place, a thing, a shift in thought or perception, or even a person. But it must always start as a deep desire within our hearts to change our present situation or feelings. Simply put, Hope is the belief that things will get better.

It starts as a tiny note in our souls and slowly rises to a thundering crescendo that can dramatically alter our circumstances and our perceptions. It can allow us to accept the present or the past and instill in us a positive outlook for our future happiness. It allows us to embrace the changes in our lives and assures us that great things can and will happen.

In short, Hope is a miracle planted inside our souls by God Almighty. We simply need acknowledge it and allow it room and time to grow. Hope, like Faith, gives us the power within to pick up the pieces of shattered dreams, desperate circumstances, loss, and uncertainty, even in our darkest of times. It is the assurance that those pieces can come together to form a magnificent, glorious future of happiness and joy.

Hope Fulfilled

by Laura Fleming Summa

I think anyone who has hoped for something has felt that dull ache in the depths of their heart. I experienced that ache for many years. My husband and I were married less than a year when we discovered I was pregnant. Before we even had time to process the thought fully, the pregnancy was over. I had miscarried. I'd never thought much about children, but now I was keenly aware of losing this little person. I would lament that I never got to hold this child. I prayed constantly, asking God to fill this void inside of me and please give me a child to love.

My journey of hope and heartache went on for seven very long years. I was pregnant six times during that time, with two of the pregnancies being twins. My heart would sink each time the doctors would tell us there was no heartbeat. We applied to be foster parents and got on lists for adoption. We even had an adoption fall through. We had just completed the nursery when my husband got the call. The young lady went into premature labor and decided to keep the baby. How absolutely crushing that news was, but things would change for us in less than six months.

We got a call from a doctor asking if we would be interested in adopting a baby. A girl was having a baby in a few weeks and was looking for a family to adopt. Within three weeks, I would hold my son in my arms. My hope was fulfilled. All those years of heartache were erased from my soul in that instant. I was somebody's Mother.

My joy would increase three years later when I gave birth to my daughter. I still hope, but now my hope is in the future. My hope will be complete when I leave the bonds of this earth and my spirit is reunited with my other eight children. I'm confident it will seem like all these years apart never happened.

Practicing Hope in God's Waiting Room

by Debra Costanzo

*B*iblically, the word "hope" is to trust in, wait for, or expect something beneficial. It's "for sure"!

In November 1969, I gave birth to a baby girl in a hospital with living accommodations dedicated to helping young girls in my situation. I decided early in the pregnancy to give my baby up for adoption. Within five days of giving birth, I had to make this decision firmly. Within three months from that date, the decision was irrevocable.

When the adoption agency came to pick up my baby, I took my first and last look at her face through the nursery window. I never held her. I never fed her. I never changed her. If I had done any of those things, I would never have been strong enough to give her up.

I thought to myself, "I will never forget her face. Never!"

My face was soaked with tears as I walked the wavy floor back to my room, unable to decipher faces as I walked past. It felt like a knife twisting in the center of my ribcage. I could not breathe.

I entered my room and closed the door behind me. I walked over to my window overlooking the Bala Cynwyd area of Philadelphia. I gazed into the blue autumn sky and asked God to reunite me with my daughter someday – even if it took thirty years. For thirty years, I prayed. For thirty years, I hoped.

On Sunday, February 28, 1999, at 8 p.m., I received a call from the adoption search agency I had registered with 2 ½ years prior. Little did I know, my daughter was also searching for me. This date is epic. It was *exactly* thirty years to the date and time that I became pregnant.

In a broken and emotional voice, the gentleman on the other end of the phone said, "I believe we found your daughter."

For thirty years, I prayed. For thirty years, I hoped. God is faithful!

Many things are possible for the person who has hope.
Even more is possible for the person who has faith.
And still more is possible for the person who knows how to love.
But everything is possible for the person who practices
all three virtues.

Brother Lawrence

H-O-P-E

Here's to Overwhelming Positive Energy

by Beth Johnston

*I*n 1964, pop star Dusty Springfield released *Wishin' and Hopin'*, one of her greatest hits. Though highly outdated, the lyrics say that you can't just "wish and hope and plan and pray (to get him into your arms)."

Wisely, the tune tells us to DO something: TELL (him), SHOW (him).... Countless times a day, the expression "I hope" is said aloud and silently. That's good. It puts great and positive energy out to the universe. Nothing wrong with that. But then what?

Life is not a spectator sport. We must turn the mere desire for an outcome into forward motion toward what it is we should never be willing to sit passively and wait for.

Have you ever hoped you would win a lottery? Did you think you could if you didn't buy a ticket? Of course not. "You have to be in it to win it."

Hoping it doesn't rain today is understandable, but none of us has control over that. Hoping you don't get stuck in the rain? Now, we have the chance to contribute to the outcome. We prepare. We carry an umbrella, and we schedule activities around weather reports.

Most importantly, we play an active role in the outcomes of our lives.

The phrase "hope springs eternal" was first coined in Alexander Pope's *Essay on Man*. It has been referenced countless times to characterize man's belief that thinking positively is good. It is!

How willing are you to look in the rearview mirror and recall how many times you "hoped"? What was your batting average on passive hoping?

Three hits out of ten at-bats get you to the Baseball Hall of Fame. Sometimes, you strike out or ground out. That's OK – you took a swing!

That's what makes you a winner!

A Scary Beginning

by Sophia Long

*A*fter COVID-19 destroyed my undergraduate career, I was over the moon to have the privilege of studying abroad. After months of preparation to move to a foreign country, I left my comfy hometown in tears; I was struggling to leave behind my family, cats, and boyfriend of four years. I would be gone for four months and was afraid of what I would face and what I would discover within myself. When I arrived at my host mom's home, I wasn't sure if I would get through the semester without my family, friends, or even a familiar language surrounding me. For weeks, I struggled to adjust to my "new life" away from home: different foods, expectations, and ways of living. I was overwhelmed by the change in culture, let alone doing university work at the same time.

About two and a half to three weeks into living abroad, I became more comfortable with my new routine. My host mom shared loads of local tips and helped me expand my knowledge of knitting. I very much enjoyed spending time with her cats, who brought me great comfort when I missed my own. I learned a few basic words in the local language and found that most people were also comfortable speaking English. I met incredible people and made friends that I anticipate will last me a lifetime – friends I plan to invite to my wedding. I traveled with those friends and also independently, visiting incredible landmarks and learning so much about how others live.

Upon embarkment, it felt like I would be there forever. But looking back, I only wish I had cherished my time abroad even more than I did. Sometimes, cherished memories have scary beginnings, and I'm learning to embrace that.

Hope itself is like a star –
not to be seen in the sunshine of prosperity
and only to be discovered in the night of adversity.

Charles Spurgeon

Hope Becomes Reality

by Sylvie Plante

After a year-long sick leave in 2009 and upon leaving the corporate world in 2014, I promised myself that I would never get sick again for a job. I started that journey by seeking freedom. Freedom of time and money. A friend introduced me to the online business world, and I immediately saw the potential for recurring and passive income. I started my first business and had some success, but nothing to write home about, which was followed by changing companies several times after that, either because I realized they were not a fit for me or they shut down.

Despite all the difficulties and the roller coaster rides I experienced (and still have), a few wonderful friends stood beside me. They supported me unconditionally during these hard times as I continued searching for a proper, professional vehicle.

There are two fundamental reasons why I want time and money freedom: 1) make a difference in people's lives every day using my skills and by doing what I love, and 2) make my health a priority. Do what I love, help others, and achieve optimal health while enjoying life to its fullest.

In July 2022, two friends introduced me to a new world and a new business I love. Aligning with my passion and achieving financial freedom is becoming a reality. Hope becomes reality.

Despite the drawbacks, the fears, the failure, and the doubts in my abilities, this journey has taught me that deep in the bottom of my heart, I knew that one day, I would find what I wanted. And I now have it! Your reality will come true if you have hope coupled with a strong conviction.

Sick of the Pain

by Angi Currier

I hoped one day the pain would either subside or dissolve completely, and though I understood we are less flexible and move more slowly as we age, but I was in my mid-40s and hurt daily!

I remember having pain in my knees as early as age 13. In 2017 and 2018, I attended my sister's wellness retreats, and my knees screamed at me. I could not do the same exercises everyone else did, like squats, lunges, or even putting pressure on my knees for push-ups. When I returned home, I started riding a stationary bike, thinking the movement would help lubricate my knee joints.

I finally decided to see the orthopedic specialists for my left knee because it was hurting worse than my right. They showed some deterioration of my bone and cartilage, and I headed down the cortisone and gel injection road to reduce inflammation. Eventually, they stopped working.

Scar tissue and bone spurs were removed during a scope. However, he diagnosed me with osteoarthritis, a deterioration of the bone, and recommended a knee replacement within two years, not the four he had anticipated.

Shortly after, my right knee began bothering me. As a single mother, I prolonged treatment as long as I could; taking time off work was not an option. The excruciating pain made it difficult to walk or perform daily activities. It was time to seek options.

I sought a second opinion with a world-renowned orthopedic surgeon. After comparing the old and new X-rays, it was apparent my knees were now bone on bone, and I needed to prevent ligament and tendon damage. In March 2023, I had a bilateral knee replacement.

I had hope in myself and confidence in my surgeon. My post-surgery pain only lasted about three weeks. Now, eight months out, I can do things I haven't been able to do for years. My quality of life is back, and I feel amazing.

May your choices reflect your hopes,
not your fears.

Nelson Mandela

Without Risk,
There is No Reward

by Tanner Willms

*M*y story, *Learning to Walk Again at 21*, was published in the *Win the Wellness W.A.R.* book in June 2023. I shared how a horrific motocross accident shattered my ankles, forcing me to relinquish my racing career and learn to walk again. After eight years of living in pain and after becoming married and a father of two active little boys, I decided enough was enough. Medical experts told me, "We have done all we can. You will have arthritis and pain for the rest of your life," I chose to take a risk and find an expert who understood. My condition was taken seriously this week, and I met someone who will change my life forever. After reviewing my x-rays, he gave me four options: fusion, partial or full ankle joint replacement, or amputation. After my visit, I wrote him this note.

Hey, Dr. Hunt,

I just wanted to reach out and personally thank you and all the staff for everything on Thursday. It really means the world. Finally, having some answers, knowing I'm not alone, and having hope for the first time in almost nine years is something I can't put into words. With that being said, I've spoken with my wife, family, and employer and feel a total ankle replacement is the best choice to take advantage of my youth and be the best I can be. I would like to expedite this process. Again, thanks to you and your team. I look forward to getting this procedure and can't wait for the future! Please reach out if you guys need anything else from me.

Follow your intuition, push for second opinions, and take risks. Especially for those of you with internal pain and suffering that no one else can visibly see, find someone who will listen, respect, and validate you. There is always hope.

Hope
HOLD ON
Pain
Ends

My Son Has Hope, So I Have Hope

by Peggy Willms

*T*anner Willms is my son. His story, *With No Risk, There is No Reward*, can be found in this book about following his intuition and pressing to find solutions for his excruciating pain after a tragic motorcycle accident in 2015 when he needed to learn to walk again at age 21. He received an answer last month that was devastating. "After an accident such as yours, your ankle is what it is." He immediately called me, "Mom, no one can see the pain I am in, and now I have no choice but to live with it."

After a short conversation and pushing him to get a second opinion, he received a life-changing call the next day. "Your ankle never healed; the bones are dying layer by layer, and we need to see you." Off to Denver, we went.

My two sons competitively raced motorcycles their whole life. One day before his fourth birthday, Tanner raced for the first time. As you can guess, any extreme sport has a high risk of injury. Between the two of them, they have had over 20 fractures and too many concussions to count.

Because they wanted to be the best at their sport, they worked hard in school, hammered the beaten desert tracks for hours on end, and pushed their talents to the limit. Every time they twisted their throttle, spewing 110 octane race gas into the air and waited for the gate to drop, they had hope. Their dedication, drive, and talent allowed them to sail across the whoop section, execute solid triple-jump landings, and be the first to nose across the finish line in many races. I had hope because they had hope.

In Tanner's story, he shares the news that a Steadman Hawkin's physician finally heard his cries. I was with him on that physician visit this week. As Tanner and I hopped on I-70 and headed west back to his hometown, for the first time in a long time, he has hope and it was palpable.

When you're at the end of your rope,
tie a knot and hold on.

Theodore Roosevelt

Where We Found Hope

by Ida Ra Nalbandian

December 2006, the doorbell rang, with a firm banging on the door. Police told us that our 17-year-old son, Vahagn, was injured as a passenger in a car driven by a drunk driver. Vahagn was in the emergency room. I nearly collapsed. The police drove us to the hospital.

Shortly after, our only child passed away. How could this be true? In agony, my mind separated from my body, tormented by intense emotional pain.

Soon, Vahagn's phone rang as his friends called to check on him. They learned of his passing and came to console us. It was our darkest hour. Even though it was late, they kept coming. We became united in pain.

Before his passing, Vahagn often asked me to buy a beaded necklace composed of wooden beads with a cross, similar to a rosary. I purchased this necklace several times. When I asked why he had me buy the same necklace repeatedly, he responded, "My friends like it, and I like giving them as gifts."

One of his friends placed that necklace on my palm that night. "You need this more than I do." After seeing my surprised look, he explained: 'Whenever one of us was going through a hard time, Vahagn handed us the necklace and said, 'Hold on to this. This will keep you strong. It helped me, it'll help you.'"

Tears rolled down my face. I began noticing many of Vahagn's friends wore that necklace. I asked what they missed most about him. "He had a vibrant and magical attitude towards everyone. He was always a genuine friend."

One day, his friends suggested creating a foundation honoring Vahagn's memory and love of music.

2007, Vahagn Setian Charitable Foundation was established with this mission:

> *Educate people about the dangers of getting*
> *into a drunk driver's car,*
> *give students musical instruments,*
> *and plant trees of hope.*

We passionately raise awareness about making mindful choices and cherish every letter of gratitude from those who benefit.

Our work builds hope that we can share with others.

Seeds of Hope

by Cyndi Wilkins

*N*ot everyone is beautiful, smart, funny, rich, or successful, but everyone is as unique as their fingerprint and has something of value to share with the world.

We all face struggles in our lives, and those born into struggle have a great deal to teach us about being vulnerable enough to ask for help when needed.

Years ago, when I had moved into my home, there was a disturbance within its walls. It was a dark, heavy energy that wreaked havoc in the night. Later, through an energetic medium, I discovered that the disturbance was an elderly man who once lived here.

He was the only son of a single parent on Welfare who grew up in the projects. He felt badly for his mother's struggles, and the local kids constantly bullied him for being poor.

By the time he came to live in my home, he was a young man with a family of his own. He always dreamed of owning his own home, and his dream came true when an uncle he barely knew left him the house in his will. However, his dream soon became a nightmare over a property dispute with his neighbors.

The "Hatfield's and McCoy's" situation continued for decades. That was his unrest, as his spirit still lingered in the home he once cherished, waiting for a resolution to his earthly squabbles.

When I asked how I could help, he suggested I plant a seed in a flowerpot and place it in a sunny area on the front porch where he loved to sit. I tended to it with loving care, and a beautiful purple flower blossomed later that summer. Purple represents spiritual wisdom and a connection to the divine.

I have not heard from him since.

*There was never a night or a problem
that could defeat sunrise or hope.*

Bernard Williams

A Space of Grace

by Gina Lobito

*A*t the beginning of Covid Shelter-in-Place, I was going through a tumultuous break-up, healing from surgery, and finding a new place to live. The stress could not have been more compounded. I felt as if my emotions had me stretched to the ends of myself while being pulled from the inside out. It was challenging to stay hopeful in the midst of my life seemingly being turned upside down.

During this time, a dear friend, Claire, was in between housing and needed a place to stay. I offered Claire the extra bedroom of the two-bedroom duplex I moved into. She graciously accepted, and I gave her a key and told her to come and go as she pleased until she found a place. I reminded her that I was in a fragile state and was not sure what kind of company I would be. I was in a deep place of healing and piecing myself back together. She understood as she was going through inner turmoil and transitions in her own life.

Every few weeks, she would leave and return for about two weeks at a time. We would gracefully navigate the shared space and occasionally have meals together. I let her know I was not myself and the cupboards were not organized and to feel free to reorganize things as she needed to. What once bothered me about having things moved around did not seem so important anymore. By the end of her stay, I told her she gave me hope. I did not think I could share life with someone again, let alone space. During our quiet and thoughtful interactions, unknown to her, she reminded me that trust, grace, patience, compassion, and love still exist. We shared a space of grace and hope.

Sending a little SUNSHINE

Healing Childhood Trauma with Ho'oponopono

by Ilene Gottlieb

*B*eing a survivor of childhood trauma, I wondered if it was possible to heal my PTSD (Post Traumatic Stress Disorder) and be free of triggers that brought up so much fear. I am grateful to share that it's possible and much easier than one might assume.

My Ho'oponopono teacher, Ihaleakala Hew Len, said: "The purpose of life is to be restored to Love... The problems are not people, places, and situations but rather the thoughts of them..."

As a child and into adulthood, when anyone touched me unexpectedly, I would experience fear. I didn't realize this was consistent with PTSD until years later. In early 2018, my fears were triggered so dramatically by an experience with my Mom that it was difficult to stay "in my body." Later that year, back pain and vertigo shut me down. During this time, I was guided to study Ho'oponopono, the ancient Hawaiian problem-solving process.

For ten years, I practiced Ho'oponopono as a guided process for clients. I repeatedly said the four phrases "I love you, I'm sorry, Please forgive me, Thank you." The ancient process was facilitated by the head of the household or local Kahuna. In the 1970s, the process was updated to what we know today, *Self I-Dentity Through Ho'oponopono*. The primary difference is that it's no longer facilitated. We are all able to do this process on our own. In essence, it's a conversation with our Creator, whom we're asking to transmute from within us all the memories or thoughts that cause our problems, whatever they are.

After healing my back pain in an hour, I focused on my PTSD and my relationship with my Mom. After four months, I realized

Ho'oponopono had been "working" when my PTSD was gone, and my Mom said, "I love you." This simple yet powerful process healed my relationship with my Mom, giving us a year and a half of loving moments before she transitioned to Spirit in 2020.

If you can say "I love you" or "Thank you," Ho'oponopono will work for you!

I Love you.
I'm sorry.
Please forgive me.
Thank you.

Ho'oponopono Prayer

Be Hopeful

Teresa Velardi

*I*n a divided world, it's easy for us to slip away from being hopeful, letting positivity fall into the shadows. May I suggest that hope is how we will be united or re-united and step back into the light?

Webster's dictionary defines **hope** as: "A desire of some good, accompanied with at least a slight expectation of obtaining it, or a belief that it is obtainable." Another online dictionary also defines it as "trust." And if I go a little deeper into hope, I find faith, and the Bible says, "Now **faith** is the substance of things hoped for, the evidence of things not seen" Hebrews 11: 1

What do you hope for? What do you have faith in? Are you hoping for a positive outcome, or are you so wrapped up in the negativity around you that you can only look at what you don't want to happen?

A simple question will open your heart to hope and abundant living: "What do I want?" Most people say, "Well, I don't want….." I know this because I've been there. Sometimes, I don't know what I want in certain situations, but I have hope and **faith** that I will know when the time is right. Hope leads to faith, and faith leads to setting positive intentions and, ultimately, an abundant life.

We need hope, or else we cannot endure.

Sarah J. Maas

Our Precious Gift of Hope

by Marla Hamann

*M*y husband and I dreamed of having a child together. I have two young men from a previous relationship, but my husband had no children, and we were trying to have a baby together.

Sadly, after an ectopic pregnancy that nearly cost me my life five weeks into the pregnancy and the loss of our second baby to miscarriage at sixteen weeks, I was depressed and hopeless.

One night, I told my husband that I didn't want to live anymore because of our failed attempts. He said, "How dare you? What about me? Your kids are having kids, so if we don't get to have any, it's okay. I have and only want you." I knew God had blessed me with my soulmate.

Two months later, after I was mentally and emotionally done and just wanted to reset, we found out we were pregnant again. After genetic testing, we were told that we were having a healthy baby girl! WHOOP WHOOP!! But, at our 20-week anatomy scan, we found out our baby girl had TAR Syndrome, Thrombocytopenia Absent Radius Syndrome. It is a rare genetic disorder characterized by the absence of the radius bone in the forearm, affecting the hands and reducing platelet count.

We weren't sure of her complete diagnosis or if she'd go full term. We researched and were told that the first two years are critical. She can live a normal life if she makes it past the second year. My Emma Layne is now two and a half, has not needed a transfusion since two months after she was born, and is holding her platelets and living her most precious life. We are happy and hopeful. I am her advocate and founded TAT (TARS Awareness Texas), a nonprofit to raise awareness and share the hope that life is possible with TARS.

Alone, we can do so little; together, we can do so much. Helen Keller

life is TOUGH but so are you

Dem Dry Bones

by M. Moses Andradé

"And he said to me, "Son of man, can these bones live?" And I answered, "O Lord God, Thou knowest" Ezekiel 37:3.

One of the most inspiring things is the first clump of crocuses tenaciously breaking through the dark, cold, wintered earth. Sometimes, even through snow. Like undaunted sentries, they remind us that Winter is almost over and Spring is drawing near.

Ah, Spring, the time of awakening, yawning, and stretching, life begins again. After a season of bitter cold and rock-hard earth, Spring speaks the promise of life emerging from death. We witness the miraculous awakening of frozen bulbs responding to a higher power calling, "Come forth."

When Ezekiel envisioned the "Valley of Dry Bones," Israel was in Babylonian captivity. Psychologically, they were depressed people, brutalized, plundered, raped, disgraced, and deported into a strange land, feeling rejected by God. The theological implications of a powerless God mocked their hopes of deliverance.

Yet, God had a plan. God excitedly bubbled over as He asked Ezekiel, "Son of man, can these bones live?" God knew what he could do for these broken people, but they needed to trust Him for their deliverance.

The whitened bones represented Israel, wintered over in defeat, sorrows, fears, and anxieties for their future; emotions and needs we are all too familiar with today. Yet, God intended to restore His people, as a nation and individuals, to bring back their joy!

Hence the question: "Can these bones live?!" Yes, weariness and grief, along with the grave clothes, can be removed at the sound of the voice of God. His invitation waits for our response. Whatever the besetting sin, God can nourish you back to health and give life to dried-up and dying faith.

Spring is here. Let the crocuses bring a smile and hopeful joy to your heart. Emerge from your death; push through the challenging circumstances and into joyfully living; glorify God. Let your life be like a *crocus* for others.

"Dem bones dem bones dem dry bones. Now hear de word o' de Lawd! 'Come forth!'"

Blessed is the man who trusts in the LORD,
and whose hope is the LORD.

— Jeremiah 17:7

Angels and Armor

Teresa Velardi

"*I* don't think I can do this anymore, God. The longer this goes on, the harder it gets to continue. But I know good will come from this, so please send an army of Angels with me as I go forward today. Thank you."

I start my day with my morning coffee, journal, and Bible app with God. That morning, I would go to court to argue my ongoing case. Feeling weary and a bit hopeless, I opened the Bible app. The day's verse was Ephesians 6:10-20, "The Armor of God." The armor is worn to stand against the forces of evil in the spiritual realm, and these verses describe the armor. I'd read this many times but was struck by the timing. I was comforted, feeling guided to move forward, knowing I had tools from a higher source.

A pastor friend sent out daily scriptures, and as I closed my journal, I saw the morning text come in. The scripture for the day was "The Armor of God." I looked up, smiled, and expressed gratitude for the reaffirmation and confidence I felt, knowing I was not alone. I went to my car with my paperwork and spiritual armor.

The drive to the courthouse was about forty minutes. I usually drive silently, gathering my thoughts, pondering my day, or reviewing my quiet time. I turned on the radio. Instead, a CD, which I didn't know was in the player, filled my car with the voice of Joyce Meyer teaching "The Armor of God."

Don't you love it when the Creator of the Universe starts the day with you, giving you hope at precisely the right time?

Hope can be a powerful force.
Maybe there's no actual magic in it,
but when you know what you hope for most
and hold it like a light within you,
you can make things happen, almost like magic.

Laini Taylor

We Found Our "One Thing."

by Dennis Pitocco

On the verge of turning 40, an unhappy Manhattan yuppie is roped into joining his two friends on a cattle drive in the southwest. On the verge of turning 40, an unhappy Manhattan yuppie is roped into joining his two friends on a cattle drive in the southwest. You may remember the famous scene in the 1991 movie "City Slickers" when Curly (Jack Palance) has the following exchange with Mitch (Billy Crystal): "One thing. Just one thing. You stick to that and the rest don't mean sh#t. But what is the one thing?" said Mitch. Curly's answer? That's what **you** have to find out."

My wife Ali and I found ours long ago — **creating more hope by doing more good**. Living a good, hopeful life is to recognize that everything and everyone matters. That includes you since you are part of the hopefulness in the world. Taking care of yourself matters. The quality of the work you do matters. It matters how you are treated and how you treat others. Each of us is a small mirror of the talents, love, and joy we have to offer each other to create our world. So, hope is energy, your positive energy, your talents, value, and your soul. It is the lifeblood of the human race. And it's not just about finding our one thing; it's about walking the talk once we found it — every day in every way.

Right now, it feels like a moment in history where choices made will have a **ripple effect** for generations to come. Whether you're a partner, friend, parent, leader, teacher, politician, or a combination thereof, it's time to show up and create more hope by doing more good to help fuel a better version of the world we live in. We did it. So can you.

One thing. **One** voice. **One** gesture. **One** uplifting word of encouragement. **One** random act of kindness. **One** ripple. Because hope matters. Because doing more good matters. Let it become your "**One** thing". Your superpower. Starting today. Starting right now. Because **YOU** matter.

ENJOY THE
simple
THINGS

Hope: The Guiding Star on the Path to Personal Fulfillment

by Brenda Warren

*F*or eight long years, I found myself stuck on a couch, consumed by my fears and insecurities due to my Post Traumatic Stress Disorder (PTSD) diagnosis. Each day felt like an uphill battle against darkness, and hope seemed like a distant dream. Little did I know that sometimes, all it takes is a glimmer of hope to ignite a fire within.

A random email would be my spark. It spoke to me, revealing how hope can be a guiding force, a beacon of light in the darkest times. With hope as my guiding star, I confronted my inner demons. Seeking therapy, surrounding myself with positive influences, and practicing self-care became my daily rituals. It wasn't easy, but with every small step forward, I grew closer to becoming the person I aspired to be.

But I didn't stop there. I realized that hope was not just meant to be experienced alone; it was meant to be shared. Inspired by the acronym H.O.P.E - Help One Person Every Day. I made it my mission to extend a helping hand to others. Volunteering to help other veterans, offering support to those in need, and spreading kindness became my purpose.

As days turned into weeks and weeks turned into months, my practice of H.O.P.E became an integral part of my everyday life. It gave me a sense of purpose and a reason to wake up each morning with a renewed sense of hope. The more I helped others, the stronger my hope grew.

My journey toward hope has taught me that even in the darkest times, there is always a glimmer of light waiting to be discovered. It is through embracing hope, extending kindness, and helping others that we can rise above our struggles and lead lives filled with purpose and joy.

Hope is not an emotion; it's a way
of thinking or a cognitive process.

Brené Brown

Paying Hope Forward

by Jeniece Paige

*I*magine moving five hours away from your family and only knowing one person. It can be a daunting and hopeless time in someone's life.

I was living in San Antonio, Texas, and met people I'm sure were angels who have shaped my life to be what it is today. During this transitional period in my life, I did not have a car in San Antonio. The bus was my means of getting to where I needed to go. I had to catch the bus everywhere.

I am grateful to have met someone who is now a very good friend, Hamid Hafizi. The man is an angel.

He loaned me his Mercedes-Benz to drive. I remember thinking, "I can't drive that car. What if something happens to it in my care?" I didn't want to be responsible for the car. But I graciously accepted the kind offer.

On the day that I started looking for a car of my own, he went with me. I found the car I wanted to purchase. I drove it for the weekend on an extended test drive. When I brought it back to the dealership, I found out that my Angel, Hamid, had purchased the car for me.

After that blessing, I wanted to share the hope that I now had for a brighter future with someone else.

I "paid the hope forward" by donating to two families for Christmas.

YOU ARE *living* ★ YOUR ★ *story*

Hope That Things Will Get Better

by Gin Yu

*I*t was the darkest of times. After putting years of effort into a relationship that wasn't receiving the priority it needed to have, it was time to walk away. It was painful and desolating. The only hope was that life didn't have to be this painful.

I sold all possessions that wouldn't fit into a Prius. I gave away anything that did not find a buyer. I quit a part-time job that was just a distraction from the dark inner monologue. I said goodbye to friends who were really just acquaintances, folks good for sharing a meal or playing board games while trying to forget everything broken in our lives. They were a momentary relief from inner despair. I said goodbye to the only creature that cared. We don't speak the same language, but it knows. There's nothing left. Only the hope that it would be better.

I traveled 2000 miles to a new beginning… again. I have lost count of how many times I've started over. This American dream had been anything but a nightmare. I was going from place to place with dreams, not goals, with no real way to accomplish them. The only hope was that things would get better.

Upon my arrival, fear and doubt crept in. What now? Then I remembered something I had heard before: "Just ask." I took out a piece of paper and jotted down a roof, a means of living. Then you are supposed to forget about it. I went to sleep, knowing things would be better. Time went by, and now I have what I asked for because that is how it works.

You create your life. But all the regrets make your soul unrestful. You want to stop the pain. You can. You give, but not to someone else. You need to give to yourself.

Give yourself the time needed to heal your wounds. Give yourself the same compassion you give others. Forgive yourself for the things that cannot be changed. You can start over at any moment once you realize that hope is knowing what's to come.

When you're at the end of your rope,
tie a knot and hold on.

Theodore Roosevelt

Find Hope in the Little Things Every Day

Teresa Velardi

*D*uring this immensely challenging time, it's essential to stay on the positive side of life, no matter how it looks on the news.

If you turn the news off, I promise you'll feel better!

Look for and find HOPE in the little things every day. Then, share it with someone you know and love who is riding the "I don't know what to feel" roller coaster called life.

Although there is much vital information to be aware of, bombarding yourself with news that can overwhelm you with fear is unnecessary and can even affect your health, both mental and physical.

Look for the good in everything and find hope every day.

Prayer is hope's breathing.
When we stop praying, we stop hoping.

— Dom Pedro Casaldaliga quoted in
Lent by Megan McKenna

*May the God of hope fill you with all joy
and peace as you trust in him.*

Romans 15:13

The God of Hope

by Donna Guary

I've taken four trips from coast to coast. In recent years, I have become afraid of flying. It has been a while since I traveled. So, you can imagine the level of anxiety I was experiencing leading up to my first flight. As each flight took off, I prayed for the aircraft, the pilots, the crew members, the passengers, and their families. *I was PRAYING!* During one flight, as I prayed, I heard, "Do you trust me?" Believing this was the voice of God and because I desire to trust Him in all things, I answered, "Yes, Lord, I trust you." To my surprise, there was a calm assurance on every flight thereafter. Like David in Psalm 23, I said, "I will not be afraid for you are with me." I learned something about myself and God that day. God promises to be with us in everything. He cares about us, and we can trust Him, and when we rest in Him, He calms our fears.

As a good Father, God wants us to trust Him in every situation, every fear, and every disappointment. We live in uncertain times, but God's promises are sure. Hoping in God will never lead us into despair. He has a vision and plan for all those who will look to Him. We can live with the assurance that He is with us to guide, protect, and restore.

Our hope in God is not dependent on getting the outcome we desire or becoming free of hardship but God's desired outcome for us. So, rest in our all-knowing God.

Now, close your eyes and bring your current situation to mind. What are you going through at this moment? Whether joyous or hardship, God loves you dearly. He's with you and promises not to leave you. Can you sense his presence? Whatever it is, the Shepherd will guide you through it. He knows what to do, and He poses the question, "Do you trust me?"

THE SUN
« always »
Shines
BRIGHTER

And Then I Met God... My Accidental Past Life Regression

by Kimberly Rinaldi

"Go back to the last time you felt safe in your body," instructed my colleague as she transitioned me back to my childhood to help me heal something I couldn't.

Next thing, I was on my deathbed. I was facing the end of my life. My four sons, their wives, children, and grandchildren were all standing around me crying. Telling me they loved me, "Mom, please don't go," they entreated. My heart broke for them, but only for a moment.

I wanted to go home. HOME. The place we all come from. The place we all return to. I was at peace. Perhaps a bit excited. I knew they'd all be good. Better than good. They were well loved and loved well.

I crossed over. I'd never felt more "ME-ness" than in that instant. I was shown two other existences and my transitions.

Each time that space in between was bliss, joy, *heaven*? It was everything in perfection at once and all potential realized; the feeling you are integral to this experience and loved beyond human measure. Knowing there is a DIVINE hand directing all that is, was, and will ever be.

And there I stood. In that space. Where I understood we are all one in this Divine Plan. We all carry that Divine Spark of Creation. I also, for a moment, felt the sadness, pain, and disappointment of my soul and every other for the atrocities we visit upon each other and ourselves.

Suddenly, the light behind me was blinding. There were sparks of gold, silver, purple, and the most glorious white shimmering light I'd ever seen.

"Turn around and tell me what you see," my hypnotherapist instructed.

I can't, I replied. I knew I was in the presence of God the way I understood him to be. God the Father and Creator; through Him, all things are made. God the Son, the Redeemer, He is our salvation. God, the Holy Spirit, is the Inspiration we have to move in the right direction for good and mutual salvation. I felt His love and acceptance. I felt compelled to turn. I did. Time ceased.

Therefore go and make disciples
of all nations, baptizing them
in the name of the Father and of the
Son and of the Holy Spirit.

Matthew 28:19

A Glass Full of Hopefulness
by Lisa Dorazio

*B*eing a positive and spirited person has always propelled me forward in life. Yet, when I lost my daughter, Christina, there were momentary lapses in my ability to remain hopeful. Nothing extreme. I never contemplated suicide because of the painful emptiness. Daily activities continued, but that numb feeling came in waves for the first few months after her passing. Intellectually, I anticipated birthing a child. Emotionally, I doubted my chances of preparing for motherhood.

Call it divine intervention – literally and figuratively – but months after my daughter's passing, I received a letter from the priest who married me. His simple letter expressing sorrow was crafted with great compassion, kindness, and understanding. It literally snapped me out of my funk. Twenty-four years later, I remember how his letter wiped the despondency from my heart, mind, and soul.

When appropriate to do so and desiring to console others, I have always reached out to others, trusting that God will help me choose appropriate words and actions. My personal goal is to spread kindness and gratitude in the world. Whether through a card, telephone call, or in-person visit, being present for a person in need is my superpower. One such example was when a woman much younger than me lost her first child – a son. Living in Canada and she in the USA, I was unable to visit her in person; however, I transported myself into her home via a greeting card. As with my experience, I learned that the card I sent her had a similarly profound effect on her and her husband. She now has two sons.

The opportunity to share kindheartedness and wisdom naturally lends itself to hopefulness. The biproduct you gain is benevolence.

It's always the season for charitableness. A lifelong commitment to being a difference-maker is my altruism. Use your thoughts, words, deeds, and even dreams to generously lavish hope in the world today!

Turning Passion into a Profession

by Linda B. Kaye

While in the Army, I met my future husband, a Captain in the Marine Corps. It was a long-distance relationship, and we got engaged over the pay telephone (for those who know what that is!). He came to Colorado, where I was stationed, for us to get married over a weekend. A few days later, we left for our honeymoon – a week of sightseeing and taking photos while driving from Colorado, Florida, and Connecticut.

When he left the Marine Corps, we moved back to Colorado. I got pregnant, but the marriage wasn't working out, and just DAYS before our daughter was born, he left. I was alone with my daughter, feeling isolated and a little hopeless as a single parent. I had to keep asking myself, "How will I support myself and my daughter?"

Money was tight, but I used the educational benefits I earned in the Army to take computer classes. Graduating first with an associate degree, I went on to earn my bachelor's in computer and management science. I embraced technology and enrolled in Pioneer Computer School of Visual Arts, where I delved into website design and desktop publishing.

I could never have imagined that someday I would be able to combine some of the skills I learned in the Army with my seemingly unrelated passion for photography, computers, and writing. All my past experiences finally came together to launch a career as a website designer.

I hoped to create a good life for us, and I did. Then, after honing my skills at a few jobs, I became my own boss. In February 2003, I launched InterActive Synergy, LLC. My website design agency is still helping clients today.

Hope lies in dreams, in imagination,
and in the courage of those
who dare to make dreams into reality.

Jonas Salk

Hope for Everlasting Life

by Tiffany Murphy

*I*t was a Saturday when I got the call that the love of my life had died in a car accident. After his transition, I cried out to God, asking Him questions because my heart yearned to know if I'd see my loved one again and if he would welcome me at the gates of heaven.

One afternoon, I felt led by the holy spirit to go see the movie *"After Death."* It was powerful. There were so many stories about people having near-death experiences and how this great warm and loving light surrounded them. They spoke about how Jesus met them at the gate of heaven. Christians, skeptics, atheists, and agnostics all witnessed this great light, each giving an account of similar experiences. I was astonished to hear that as they stood at heaven's gate, their loved ones met them there and welcomed them home.

This movie gave me so much peace, hope, and joy, knowing that if I live according to God's Word, I hope to see those I love again. This world is temporary, but I have hope to live again in the eternal presence of Jesus Christ. I hope not only will I make it into heaven, but my best friend will welcome me with open arms, stating, "Welcome home."

The movie helped me see the light of Jesus and how bright it is that even when life gets hard, I have eternal hope. To know that to leave this body is to be in the presence of the Lord. What's better than that? This world has time for joyful occasions and happy moments, but the greatest hope is to be in the presence of Jesus for eternity.

In His presence is the fullness of joy forevermore (Psalm 16:11).

There is no way to get to heaven to see your loved one except through your faith in Jesus Christ.

For those who have experienced loss, God can help you have eternal hope.

I Have Prayed for You

M. Moses Andradé

Simon! Simon! Behold, Satan has demanded permission to sift you like wheat, but I have prayed for you that your faith fail not (Luke 22:31-32)

Christ and his disciples had just finished the Passover meal. Several events leading up to his crucifixion were about to unfold. He was to be betrayed by Judas, forsaken by the disciples, and falsely accused by the Jewish religious leaders. Yet, Christ's concern was for Peter as He assured him, "I have prayed for you."

Satan once demanded and was given consent to "sift" Job. He was severely assaulted, but though Job cursed the very day of his birth, he did not recant his faith in God.

A similar battle raged in both Peter and Judas and rages about us today! Satan desires us to compromise our faith in God and lose hope. He strikes our weakest areas, bringing discouragement, hopelessness, doubt, guilt, and confusion as he did to Peter and Judas.

Then, when the darkness of anti-faith emotions overwhelms us, and we don't let go and let God hold us, Satan seeks to destroy us. Just as he wrapped Judas and Peter in the darkness of his lies, he will attempt to deceive us.

Judas and Peter discovered that the weakest area of our lives is where God is strongest. We must accept Christ's promise: "I have prayed for you that your faith fail not." (Luke 22:32).

Our faith in God's promises, coupled with the principles of His righteousness, will take us through the dark hours of temptations and life's hardships, no matter how crushing. Christ will lead us, but we must have the faith to trust and follow Him.

While there's life, there's hope.

Marcus Tullius Cicero

Life is Full of Hope

by Sandra Kitt

I woke up after three weeks with a brain injury and was unable to move, talk, or swallow. When I was in the middle of this battle for survival, hope became a luxury that never crossed my mind. Every minute was consumed with tests, therapies, and adjusting to a new life. Most of my time was spent just trying to get through the day.

Then, one day in therapy, I saw a poster for the National Disabled Veterans Winter Sports Clinic. It showed a quadriplegic skiing down a mountain in Aspen, Colorado. It caught my attention since I skied in Europe in the Army.

It took over two years before I was well enough to join over 400 disabled veterans from across the country. I was very nervous at first, but it was the most inspirational experience of my life. Going up the ski lift, I saw blind and quadriplegic veterans skiing down an 11,000-foot mountain.

Standing at the top of the mountain looking down, I realized anything was possible with the right equipment and support. This experience gave me hope to see others like me courageously overcome their limitations.

As part of the weeklong event, we participated in other winter sports. During five different trips, I've had the opportunity to snowmobile, cross-country ski, play sled hockey, and try curling. These experiences have inspired me to travel and participate in other sports, such as recumbent bike riding, scuba diving, and sky diving. All these activities helped me understand that life is still full of HOPE, even when life looks different.

It Is Written

by M. Moses Andradé

"*I*t is written!" Three simple words. Christ responded to Satan's temptations in the wilderness with "It is written."

When tempted, Christ also provides "a way out" (I Corinthians 10:13 NIV). In Matthew 4:4, 7, 10, *It is written* echoes a theme of truth, a strategy to find a way out by looking for God's counsel, trusting, and depending on God.

Will this work for us today? Yes, but we must decide to take that first step toward Jesus to experience faith. His example to fortify His mind with Scriptures, and so must we become skilled at knowing how and when to reference the sacred text.

Temptation is the rationale presented to abandon God's code of righteousness - to sin. The counter-argument "It is written" is the reason not to sin. *It is written* represents the Word of God that requires our total trust and obedience. Following the Word is more than memorization; it allows the message to enter your thinking until your innermost thoughts reflect God. With David, we can say, "Your Word of truth and guidance have I treasured so deeply in my heart, that I will not rationally seek an occasion to willfully sin against You." (Psalm 119:11).

Can you remember when you applied the "It is written" to challenges in your life? We need a store of Scripture knowledge translated into principles to face each day's onslaught. Satan is a subtle enemy, crafty and deceptive, and we are easy prey unless we read God's Word and meet Him personally. Getting acquainted with God's precious Word begins our defense against weakening temptations. Little by little, we must digest the Word, for we have life and hope in them. Remember,

"Man shall not live by bread alone" but man lives by everything that proceeds out of the mouth of the Lord (Deuteronomy 8:3; Christ's paraphrase Matthew 4:4). It only takes consecrated dedication, time, and desire to receive the Holy Spirit, who will help and enable you as you prevail over temptations. He has promised never to leave or forsake us.

Claim the promise, "I can do all things through Christ who strengthens me" (Philippians 4:13). "It is written" is our defense and hope in our challenges.

With man this is impossible,
but with God all things are possible.

Matthew 19:26

My Fifteen Year Hope Filled Journey

by Carolyn Ballenger

*I*collaborated in Ohio with Diane Gee to write a song about 15 years ago to be sung by the children in our church's YES (Youth Expressing Spirit) Dept. We were going to make a CD as a fundraiser but never did.

Several years later, while in San Diego, the song was to be used for a Multi-Religious International Children's Choir. This song, Spirit Lives, was perfect for this event since it stated, Spirit lives in me, Spirit lives in you, and Spirit lives in us. Our choir dropped out, and the song didn't get used.

I was disappointed and felt like our words and the song we created would never be shared. I know-things happen in Kairos time (God's Time) and not Chronos time (our time). So I continued to be grateful for each delay and every NO, knowing that it would lead to an even bigger YES when I opened and allowed myself to be led from the heart.

Fast forward ten years to Covid. As my Ordination project, I got the chance to create music videos with my current YES (Youth Expressing Spirit). I sent an email asking the New Thought singers I knew if they would sing one of my songs. John Stringer was the first musician to say "YES. " He then invited Karen Drucker to sing with him. These are two powerhouse musicians in the positive music circle. They collaborated, our kids learned some choreography, and we created an inspirational music video with this song.

Spirit had a much bigger plan for this song than I could have ever imagined. This project gave me hope that things are always working in the background for our greater good. View the video here: https://bit.ly/spiritlives

Hope sees the invisible, feels the intangible, and achieves the impossible.

Helen Keller

The Layers of Hope

by Mark Reid

*I*n the bitter cold of January 2002, I left my job in Vermont, packed up my little Toyota, and chased love across the country to Los Angeles, California. I was filled with hope! Within a week of my arrival, my world crumbled. I discovered betrayal—the woman I loved had been cheating. Heartbroken, I spent six months futilely mending my wounds. So, in the scorching heat of summer, I summoned hope once more, and moved again across the U.S. to West Palm Beach, seeking solace with a friend who, unbeknownst to me, harbored ulterior motives.

What was tragedy in L.A. escalated into a Florida nightmare. My roommate-turned-stalker invaded my work, shadowed my every move, and watched me sleep at night. Fleeing seemed the only option yet again in my young life. Reluctant to ever "quit" anything, I was at my wit's end. Nevertheless, I embarked on a journey across the globe, landing a job teaching English in South Korea. Once the paperwork finalized, I boarded a plane and embraced the unknown. Still filled with hope.

In 2003, amidst the vibrant landscapes of South Korea, my life transformed. That year became a testament to resilience and new beginnings. My story isn't an advocacy to simply flee from life's problems; I initially strove to navigate my way through both dismal situations.

The moral here resonates in the layers of hope. Even when my first grand hope shattered, and the subsequent hope crumbled, a reservoir of hope persisted.

I opted for a radical shift, transcending international borders to start anew. But, behind every setback, hope endured like flickering candlelight behind despair. The critical component in getting through the muck of life is to never allow hope to perish. Hope persists in layers, waiting to be rediscovered over and over again when necessary.

One of the toughest years of my life was followed by one of the best. That's just how hope works sometimes. Hope prevails unless we surrender to despair.

Fall down seven times,
get up eight.

Japanese Proverb

Hope for Healing Our Hearts and Our Land

Jessie Tieva

*P*eople often ask why I live in Minnesota. I've traveled to 38 countries, lived in England and Mexico, visited every state in the USA, and lived in four. Why I chose to live in "the tundra" with a short window of warm weather is shocking to some. The weather is my favorite part; I love the change of seasons, but harvest time is short for my family garden.

When I look at and cradle my child, my precious little Abel, helpless and resting, all I see is love. He is a shining light of love and hope in a world that said he wasn't "compatible," and I've learned so much from him.

I choose not to be compatible with today's politics in this season of change. I won't change anyone's mind with a vote or a yard sign. But I can make a difference with love and prayer. People are looking for solutions to the hurt in the wrong places. Posting inflammatory outrage isn't going to "fix" anything. The only solution, answer, or way back is love. I hope we can seek forgiveness and heal through the power of love.

I won't be part of the noise anymore. I want to be part of the solution. Let's heal families, friendships, and hearts with love. The harvest is ripe in this season of change to heal relationships and hearts through love and maybe a pumpkin spice latte. I think that is how real change happens.

> *"If my people, which are called by my name,*
> *shall humble themselves, and pray, and seek my face,*
> *and turn from their wicked ways; then will I hear from heaven,*
> *and will forgive their sin, and will heal their land."*

2 Chronicles 7:14

Hope Floats

by Lara Scriba

*T*hirteen years ago, my husband and I boldly decided to embark on a life of adventure and simplicity, trading our traditional home for the gentle sway of a sailboat, setting a course for a life afloat. We wanted our children to experience the wonders of connection, curiosity, and a sense of belonging to something greater than themselves.

Our faith in humanity is renewed as we navigate the open waters and encounter new faces. The acts of kindness bestowed upon us by strangers remind us that compassion knows no boundaries. Together, we share our passions and guide our children, imparting skills to survive and the wisdom to thrive as compassionate human beings.

Living in constant motion offers our children a unique opportunity to discover themselves. They learn to embrace the ever-changing environment, finding solace in the unpredictability of nature. Each sunrise and sunset, the ebb and flow of the tides, the shifting seasons - these rhythms become their guideposts.

In this dance with nature, our children learn to find their place in the world on their own terms, understanding the importance of following their passions and stepping off the beaten path. They discover the power of joy and the courage to pursue what makes them feel alive.

Our life afloat has become a tapestry of experiences woven together by the threads of adventure and resilience. We have chosen a path less traveled, and in doing so, we have discovered a world filled with inspiration and endless possibilities.

So, as we continue to sail toward the horizon, we hold onto our dreams for our children. We believe that by immersing them in the beauty of this world, they will grow into compassionate, curious, and resilient individuals. And with each passing day, our hope for their future shines brighter, for we know they are destined for greatness on their own unique journey.

Never give up. Expect only the best from life and take action to get it.

Catherine Pulsifer

A Grateful Heart is a Hopeful Heart

Teresa Velardi

L iving in gratitude will help you find the way through whatever is before you.

It's been said that 'what we think about, we bring about.' So, it's up to you as to what life holds for you. Living with a grateful heart brings hope into the unknown and sometimes scary situations that life can hand us.

When these times lead you into fear, did deep into your heart to find gratitude for something, anything, even if you think there is nothing for which to be grateful. Gratitude is not something you *think*. Being grateful is a *feeling*. Once you have it, hold on to that grateful feeling and watch hope rise with it.

Ultimately, when you consistently find people, places and things to be grateful for, the feeling of hopefulness will be consistently part of your day to day living.

Then, watch for the blessings!

What oxygen is to the lungs,
such is hope to the meaning of life.

Emil Brunner

A Tale of the Cowardly Lion

by Mark Thomas Heidt

I do believe in ghosts; I do believe in ghosts.
I do, I do, I do, I do believe in ghosts.

The Cowardly Lion, Wizard of Oz

*H*ope is not pleading. The Lion, trusting only in himself, let fear take control and appeased the Wicked Witch by believing in her power to save him.

The foundation of hope is trust, a belief that the one we are trusting will come to our rescue or fulfill our desire. The enemy understands that fear, subjecting us to terror, often makes us trust their power to end the threat.

That doesn't work. Seeing your fear, the enemy doubles down the attack. The Wicked Witch replied to the Lion, "Ah! You'll believe in more than that before I'm finished with you."

The answer is to place our trust in God. Throughout the Bible, the common theme is "Trust in the Lord your God with all of your heart." When we place our hope and trust in God, relying on HIS faithfulness instead of ourselves, we experience His Grace, mercy, goodness, and love. Unlike the Witch, God wants to, and will fulfill our desire, most importantly, our rescue and salvation.

Fear distracts from the main objective, which for the Lion was to obtain courage. " Have I not commanded you? Be strong and coura-geous. Do not be afraid; do not be discouraged, for the Lord your God will be with you wherever you go." (Joshua 1:9). When we 'get out of ourselves' putting our trust in God, we get refocused and empowered for victory.

Then Lion would have prayed, "I will say of the LORD, He is my refuge and my fortress: my God, in whom I trust. I shall not be afraid" (Psalm 91); then "Ghosts be cast out!!" Now, that's hope bolstered by courage!

Move from fear and self-reliance to trust in God and His Word; He will deliver the substance you have hoped for and believed in.

Our new "courageous" Lion, after his prayer, the Wicked Witch will be fleeing the forest saying, "Angels and Lions and God, oh my!"

For our light and momentary troubles are
achieving for us an eternal glory that far
outweighs them all. So we fix our eyes not on
what is seen, but on what is unseen,
since what is seen is temporary,
but what is unseen is eternal.

2 Corinthians 4:17-18

There is Always
Hope — Even in our Deepest Fear

Teresa Velardi

There was a time in my life when I felt I was relentlessly being punished by God for decisions I made while clearly knowing in my heart He had warned against them. It took a long time for me to find my way back to God and recognize who I am in the eyes of the Creator of All Things.

This piece by Marianne Williamson helped me have hope for my future, let go of the fear, step into my faith and for the first time in my life, trust God and know that He loves me. He loves you too!

"Our deepest fear is not that we are inadequate.
Our deepest fear is that we are powerful beyond measure.
It is our light, not our darkness, that most frightens us.
We ask ourselves, 'Who am I to be brilliant, gorgeous,
talented, fabulous?'
Actually, who are you not to be?
You are a child of God.
Your playing small does not serve the world.
There is nothing enlightened about shrinking so that other people
won't feel insecure around you.
We were all meant to shine, as all children do.
We were born to make manifest the glory of God that is within us.
It's not just in some of us, it's in everyone.
And as we let our own light shine, we unconsciously
give other people permission to do the same.
As we are liberated from our own fear, our presence liberates others."

Marianne Williamson: *A Return to Love*

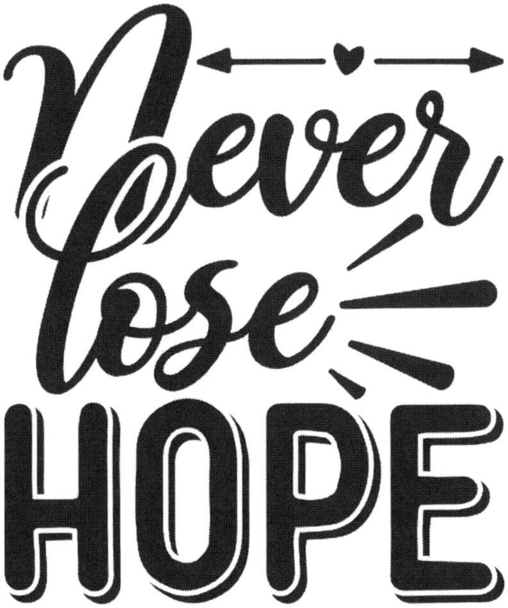
Never
lose
HOPE

Let Hope Transform You

Charla Anderson

*H*OPE. It's such a simple word, yet it carries immense power and echoes the resilience of the human spirit. A life without hope is like a bird without wings- stagnant, demoralized, condemned to a bleak existence. Hope is our safe haven in the storm, a beacon that lights up our darkest night, promising brighter days.

Gratitude is at the core of hope. In times of adversity, acknowledging our blessings keeps our spirits buoyant and fuels our journey onward. The more grateful we are, the more hopeful we become. Much like a flower turning towards the sun, gratitude encourages us to look for the positive and beauty around us.

Bold faith is a requisite companion of hope. It takes courage to have faith - to believe in something unseen, to trust that a higher plan shapes our purpose. Bold faith propels us to leap into the unknown, overcome obstacles, and, most importantly, maintain hope.

No story of hope is complete without overcoming challenges. Hope transforms us in the thorny path of trials, and we evolve from weakness to strength. Overcoming these difficulties strengthens us and solidifies our unshakeable belief in a better future.

Remember that whatever you say after the words "I AM" is WHO YOU ARE! Every. Word. Matters. Remember to speak what you *want*, not what you don't want. Speak *life*. Speak *health*. Circumstances don't define you! And you are loved and worthy. Love yourself enough to receive it.

Hope enriches our lives, empowers us with resilience, and gives us a worldview that says, "Never give up." Embed gratitude in your life, pursue a bold faith, conquer your challenges, and let the magic of HOPE transform you.

*The road that is built in hope is more pleasant to the traveler
than the road built in despair,
even though they both lead to the same destination*

Marion Zimmer Bradley

Special Delivery (Part 1)
by Will Pollock

Suzette walked in the front door, cradling Raffi in a blanket, and placed her in my son's lap. "Here's your new baby sister, Cam!" Overjoyed with surprise, Cam hugged a very stiff, scared puppy who was unsure of her new surroundings.

Raffi—a gorgeous, 10-month-old Rat Terrier rescue we adopted out of Texas—made a long journey via volunteer shuttle and multiple stops to get to us in Atlanta. After losing our precious furbaby, Triscuit, the year prior, we were ready to open our hearts and love a new four-legged friend.

After Suzette departed and the three of us were alone, our exuberance turned to stress. Every time I tried to leash her, Raffi would run away. She would pee on the floor if I even moved in her direction. I couldn't even crate her because she was too scared by her new surroundings, which led me to think she'd been neglected or worse, abused.

The next day, behavioral experts came over and coaxed her with high-value treats. Slowly, Raffi emerged from hiding and started interacting with us. Later, we tried hug therapy and verbal affirmations with some success. I felt hopeful we could turn the ship around and "breakthrough" Raffi's shock of new surroundings and humans.

What emerged during the intervening weeks, sadly, was a gentle soul slowly learning potty training and bonding with me, her human, while remaining reactive to my son.

One afternoon, the three of us were playing in the den, and after Cam did one of his silly moves, Raffi went up and nipped him on the hand. At that exact moment, I knew the situation called for switching to foster parenting and finding Raffi a new home, without kids, where she could thrive.

Hope, at that moment, felt like a complex abstraction 500 miles away. But little did I know a new joy was right around the corner.

Special Delivery (Part 2)

by Will Pollock

*R*affi's new adoptive family and I were sitting in the living room, chatting about her talents.

"She's doing great with potty training and vocabulary," I beamed. "And she loves standing on her hind legs to give hugs. Watch!" I called Raffi over, put my hands up, and said, "Hugs!" She immediately stood up and clasped her front paws around my hands.

My rapport with Raffi—which we manifested together after working through nerves and fear—was about to end. I felt sad but resolute that Raffi was about to change a new family's life forever.

At departure time, I picked Raffi up and tucked her in the travel crate with her blanket and a treat. "Love you, sweet girl," I said. As they departed the house, I felt a mix of emotions, from hope and pride to sadness and loss.

A few months on, my son started asking about a new puppy. And I, too, felt a spark that it was time to start looking again. We were keen on another Terrier, and we wanted to adopt. This time, I wanted Cam with me during adoption instead of surprising him so we could feel the hope of adding to our family together.

After looking at dozens of profiles, I stumbled on "Clyde" from North Georgia Humane. A 10-month-old Fox Terrier mix, he was handsome and mischievous, much like my 4-year-old. I was sold, and Cam was too.

After completing the application, I started a great conversation with Debbie Barton, the rescue coordinator. A few hours later, Debbie called me and said, "I just know in my heart this is right, so you're approved!" Cam and I drove north to meet and pick up Clyde—now called Jackson—and the rest, as they say, is history.

When Raffi's mom got wind of our new family member, she sent Jackson a goody bag filled with toys and treats.

Building hope was a team effort.

Most of the important things in the world have been accomplished by people who have kept on trying when there seemed to be no hope at all.

Dale Carnegie

A Trail of Hopeful Words of Wisdom

Teresa Velardi

*I*f you look at life from a new vantage point — a new perspective, you may find hope in places you never thought it might exist.

There is much wisdom and hope in the words of Steve Jobs. These are just some tidbits he left for us to ponder, learn, and grow from. There are many more in his Stanford Commencement Address in 2005.

Do you see the hope in these words? Lean in and read with the eyes of your hopeful heart.

> *Believe that things will work out.*
> *Follow your intuition and curiosity.*
> *Trust your heart, even when it leads you off the*
> *well-worn path.*
> *You have to trust that the dots will somehow*
> *connect in your future.*
> *The only way to do great work is to love what you do.*
> *Have the courage to follow your heart and intuition;*
> *they somehow already know what you*
> *truly want to become.*
> *Everything else is secondary.*

Steve Jobs

The moment you doubt whether you can fly,
you cease forever to be able to do it.

J. M. Barrie

"Breath of HOPE: A Symphony of Strength"

by Sally Mary S de Leon

Some moments in the symphony of life echo with pain, resonating deep within our chests and bellies. The ache extends from our heads to our hearts, creating a storm that threatens to engulf us. Yes, this moment is undeniably painful, but within it lies a transformative power—a power rooted in HOPE.

This pain is but a fleeting note in the grand composition of our existence. It is a momentary shadow cast by the brilliance of our inner strength. We must remember, amidst the throbbing discomfort, the fortitude that resides within us. This is not the end; it is merely a chapter—a brief interlude in our life's epic tale of resilience.

Take a breath, not just any breath, but a deliberate inhale and a slow, controlled exhale. In the rhythm of your breath, discover the cadence of HOPE. Each breath is a reminder that you can navigate through the storms to weather the tumultuous seas of uncertainty. Inhale strength, exhale doubt.

As you breathe, envision HOPE as a force transcending the present moment. It is a beacon, guiding you through the darkness towards a future bathed in the warm hues of possibility. With each breath, you are not merely inhaling air; you are inhaling the promise of a brighter tomorrow.

This is a testament to the indomitable spirit within you. The pain may linger, but so does your resilience. It's a journey, and in the grand tapestry of your life, this moment is but a single stitch. Hold onto HOPE as if it were a brush, painting vibrant strokes of courage and optimism onto the canvas of your story.

Yes, the pain is real, but so is the strength that courses through your veins. With every breath, you are not just surviving; you are thriving. Embrace the discomfort, for on the other side lies a landscape adorned with the blossoms of HOPE, a testament to the enduring strength within you.

Happiness: Cultivate joy in every moment;

Openheartedness: Approach life with an open and loving heart;

Positivity: Foster a constructive and optimistic mindset;

Endurance: Persist with resilience and fortitude.

Letting Go of Judgment
Embracing Hope

Teresa Velardi

*A*re you kidding? A cardinal? That woman is out of her mind!

The woman said God was watching over her whenever she saw a red cardinal. I judged that she was out of her mind.

My religious upbringing taught me about a vengeful, punishing God. I decided that God didn't love me anymore, and I was being punished. That's why my life was such a mess, and I wasn't going to God with any of the hurt and pain plaguing my life. I was miserable!

One morning, while walking, I finally cried out to God. I was desperate, hopeless, and had nothing to lose. With tears streaming down my face, I asked for a sign that God was with me and that I could still turn to Him.

I heard a little peep of a bird, one I was familiar with. There was a red cardinal in the majestic red maple tree in our front yard! Seriously? I remember saying out loud, "Very funny, God!" I think I even heard a little giggle inside.

At that moment, I renewed my relationship with God and began to trust again. With gratitude, I let go of the judgment of the cardinal story. Ironically, cardinals have been with me ever since and have been a symbol of hope. They nested in that tree for years. They appeared in the apple tree outside my bedroom window when I moved.

There are many opinions and meanings connected to these beautiful birds. I believe they are a little bit of heaven: a whisper from God and a wink from my parents.

God is good!

STARS CAN'T *shine* without darkness

The Healing Power of Hope and Art

by Sharon Durbin Graves

I began an art career after being rejected for a double lung and heart transplant over twenty years ago. I was sent home and told to get my affairs in order, and I decided that I would learn to paint since I already had my affairs in order.

I always felt like there was an artist inside of me, but life got in the way for a season. I was married, had a full-time job, owned businesses, and had four children, so learning to paint was pretty far down on my list of things I wanted to accomplish.

When I realized that my time was probably now limited, I went at it full force with all the hope that I would have enough time to learn a few things and create a piece or two of art I liked.

I had the hope of seeing my youngest child graduate from high school. I had the hope of seeing another grandchild be born. But I also had a nagging sense that there was an artist inside of me, and I hoped to bring that out.

Doctors did not give me hope. I had that hope inside of me that regardless of what their plans were for me, I had my own plans, and that did not include dying at the age of 48. So I painted. I did everything I could to bring the artist out in me that I just knew was hiding deep inside.

Giving up was never an option for me, even when all I produced was crap. But finally, I began to improve, which was all the proof I needed to keep going. Keep going! Keep at it.

It's always something,
to know you've done the most you could.
But, don't leave off hoping,
or it's of no use doing anything.
Hope, hope to the last.

Charles Dickens

Hope and Abundant Faith

by Gloria Sloan

*H*ope latches on to faith, helping us brave life's uncertainties. Hope provides a feeling of expectation for our desires and beliefs. It merges with faith for aspiration and anticipation.

The Bible is clear on the teachings of hope and our faith's affirmation. When we try to live by the doctrine set before us, the path of hopeful righteousness is our shield. The power of the Holy Spirit leads us. The classic biblical story is when Mary developed hope after a visit from the angel Gabriel about giving birth to Jesus (Luke 1:26-38). She was told not to be afraid because she had found favor with God. She was confused and disturbed, but the angel gave her hope and said, "The Lord is with you!" Her circumstances were unbelievable and, above all, uncertain. Yet, throughout the story, Mary remains strong with hope and unwavering faith.

Mary was known to mediate and keep things she pondered close to her heart. Although shocked and in fear of this supernatural experience, she held on to her hope and abundant faith as she submitted to God's will. I can only imagine her honorable response as her life unfolded with hope and greatness. God wants us to develop this kind of hopefulness revealed by faith for our future dreams and aspirations.

What brings you hope? Think about your enthusiastic purpose in life that provides a sense of meaning and achievement. Hope is essential to motivate our positive actions and strengthen our faith, which will lead to positive results. Hope can help relieve stress, improve our relationships, and broaden our mindset. Hope can make us happier and reinforce our abundant faith.

The foundation of spiritual well-being is driven by hope, one of the three gifts mentioned by the apostle Paul in (1 Corinthians 12:4). The privilege to possess this amazing gift is beyond God's ultimate goodness. Hope is a blessing to cherish forever.

A Manifestation Journey Fueled by Hope

by Fran Asaro

*H*ope is not a word I frequently use in my vocabulary. It's not a 'bad' word. Still, for someone like me, who has spent decades honing strong manifestation skills, my language revolves around phrases like 'causing a result,' 'intentionality,' 'being deliberate,' and 'creating.'

It's more about partnering with God for results rather than simply hoping for a favorable outcome. This means I have a role to play. My part is to stay focused, ensure I align with my worthiness, harbor pure, loving intent, and trust that God will provide.

Do I achieve everything I set out to manifest? Well, no. I'm still a work in progress and probably will be for life. But I've found that I attain better results now, more than ever. Once I realized I am not a victim, there is no need to beg for anything, and others aren't inherently more worthy than I am, things unfolded organically.

I live my life with gratitude for everything I have. I strive to remain in that place as often as possible, more than in the state of 'asking.' However, I need essential things to live comfortably, like a safe home, having my basic needs met, and I aspire to make a difference in this world. I can't do that alone, for sure. I rely on God's assistance for all of these and so much more.

While not my central focus, hope still plays a pivotal role in my journey. It's the initial belief that brighter days are possible, serving as a driving force that encourages me to take action and co-create my desired reality. So, even though I may prefer other words, hope remains a vital thread woven into the fabric of my manifesting journey.

We must accept finite disappointment,
but never lose infinite hope.

Martin Luther King, Jr.

Hope: Light in Our Dark
by Kathleen (Kat) O'Keefe-Kanavos

So often, we feel so alone. We are sure no one else has experienced our crisis or feelings, so there is no hope for help. Reading how someone else experienced a similar life challenge and survived the devastation helps us keep walking through the storm one more day.

In High School, my favorite song in chorus was the 1963 hit *You'll Never Walk Alone*, by Gerry and the Pacemakers. Many crooners, including Elvis Presley, have since sung it. These lyrics still resonate with me because they exemplify hope in our darkness:

> *Walk on through the wind*
> *Walk on through the rain*
> *Though your dreams be tossed and blown*
> *Walk on, walk on*
> *With hope in your heart*
> *And you'll never walk alone...*

Winston Churchill said, "If you're going through hell, keep going," and then discussed the "Lion Heart" of all people. We have all gone through some form of hell, myself included, but rather than giving up when doctors told me I had advanced cancer recurrence, I kept going and embraced my Lion Heart, followed hope forward until I came out the other side of my darkness and into hope's light.

The dark hour of our soul can become the fertile ground to grow our Miracle of Hope. Without one, the other cannot exist.

A belief in Divine Intervention can trigger hope and make the difference between life and death. Here is how it all works. Miracles of Hope grow when we peer back through the dark from a place of light. Wisdom shared with others makes us beacons of light and hope during their storm. Hope is the light in our dark hour that guides us through the storms in life. *Walk on with HOPE in your heart...*

Weather the Storm

by Sandra Heidt

Whenever I face an unexpected challenge in life, I remember the story my father-in-law George told me.

One sunny day, George took three yacht club members and their children, including his son Mark, my future husband, for an afternoon sail on Long Island Sound on his sailboat. Suddenly, as would happen on the Sound, a violent storm arose.

Curious, I asked what he did, and George said, "The first thing is set your eyes **off** the impending doom and instead **focus** on the substance of faith, the outcome you see by hope, that being safely enduring the storm. Next, you pray for wisdom, knowing what to do when you don't know what to do. Then, with my focus on the hope of safety, wisdom arrived. My sailing instructor said, 'If you encounter a storm, don't run away; it will catch up. Don't turn sideways. It will blow you over; instead, steer the boat directly into the storm and keep going to make it through.' And indeed, we made it through unharmed."

He said, "My point is when you face challenges in life, first don't be moved by what you see. Instead, be moved by faith and hope. Instead of the emotion of fear, bring forth the 'spiritual' joy of seeing/experiencing a happy outcome. But don't think you can do it on your own. Pray for God to give you wisdom, which he has promised in his Word, and he will. Then, with wisdom, act with all your strength and courage. Most importantly, don't run from the challenges. Run head on, and press on till you achieve victory."

Of course, I had to ask, "What if the storm sank the sailboat?"

He replied, "I never considered that outcome; I never lost hope. But if it did sink, I wouldn't blame God for not answering my hope by my chosen method – sailing through the storm. Instead, in faith and hope, once overboard, my prayer would have been, 'Lord, teach us to walk on water; it's too far to swim."

*Let us hold unswervingly to the hope we profess,
for He who promised is faithful.*

— Hebrews 10:23

Hope Changed My Life

by Sharlene R. Prince

I sit here looking out the window as tears overwhelm me and slowly run down my cheek. As I reflect, I realize that sometimes, we allow others to dictate and control our path, even when they do not comprehend our goals and dreams.

I remember something kept pushing me to go back to school to obtain my master's degree. I wanted that for myself, even more so when people kept telling me I would not make it through. There are times when those words resonate with you and make you hopeless.

When I spoke with my mom, she said, "Don't you think you are a little too old to go back to school? It will be hard for people your age."

I was thirty-four years old. I suddenly started to doubt myself and my capabilities.

Deep down inside, I had to prove her wrong, so I registered for the following semester. There was this gnawing feeling inside of me that said I could do it. I was hopeful that I could conquer this fear that was developing into knots in my belly.

I stayed quiet in the background in every class to avoid being caught off guard by a question I was unprepared to answer. Then it happened: my professor called on me, and for a moment, I was stumped, as all eyes were on me. I was hopeful and stayed positive as I began to answer the question' as I started speaking, all eyes were on me, and heads began to nod in agreement.

Anybody who knows me knows I couldn't stop talking once I began. I passed all my classes and graduated. Moving forward, I promised always to stay hopeful in completing my goals.

Never Give Up on You!

The best IS YET TO Come

Finding Hope in
Troubled Waters

by Janice Silva

I have been thinking a lot about hope lately. I often say I am in the hope-dealing business. It is a word that has meant something to me all my life.

My daily mantra lately is as follows: I am in my right place, at the right time, with the right people for the right purpose.

I am safe. I am here. I am enough.

When I stay in this place of understanding, I feel hope. I have made friends with hope, and I like to call her to my side, in times of trouble.

I believe we, as one humanity, come from the same One Source. I see hope as one of our Source-given qualities that help us remain grounded and connected in the winds of turbulence.

We all feel the winds of turbulence. There is no way around them. I am grateful to my parents for the strong foundation they gave me from birth in the power of Love. If they were still here, they would tell me, we are so proud of you, and we are with you, cheering you on. Feeling them with me, from that special place beyond that we cannot see with these eyes, helps me remain steadfast in my hopeful understanding that Love will help us all find our way in the dark.

We are all in our right place at the right time, together now, for the right purpose. I see that purpose as helping humanity rise above the clouds and stay centered in Source through sharing my experience, strength, and hope.

I dwell in possibility.

Emily Dickinson

To Have Faith, You Must Have Hope

by Patricia Dolce

*H*ope is the driving force in our search for daily comfort and content. We all wish for a successful marriage, success for all our family, especially our children and grandchildren, and good health for all. These wishes or hopes also extend to our friends. We all know that when someone feels that one or more of our hopes and wishes are dashed, either by the death of a loved one, failed relationships, bad decisions, or other unexpected disappointments in life, hope fades, and faith goes with it.

I have been blessed to have a very dear friend for over thirty years. Unfortunately, at some point in time, she lost all faith and hope and succumbed to a deep depressive state. Ultimately, the depression manifested in declining physical and mental health.

Although I am not a medical professional, I provided comfort and hope when needed. It was just simple things that she needed and that I could provide. Examples: going shopping, a trip to our favorite restaurant, including her in our traditional family get-togethers. We made great progress together; she became her old self and was preparing to resume her daily routines. I believe that her health was improving, and her mental state was allowing her to have hope that things would change for the better. It was great to have my good friend back for a while. I hoped things would continue for the better, but something must have triggered a decline again.

My phone calls, cards, and letters were going unanswered. Nothing I tried was working. I had lost my friend once again. I hope we can someday reconnect so that I may have the opportunity to help restore her faith. I believe that she has once again lost all hope. I keep her in my thoughts and prayers and have faith and hope that one day, she will get better.

Hope Found Me

by Amanda Gust

For almost a decade, I wandered about searching for hope in all the wrong places. I searched for hope in the bottom of a glass of wine. Sometimes, I would look for hope in a steaming hot bath with the lights dimmed low. Most of the time, I sought to fill my hope with people. Maybe, just maybe, if I placed hope in a new partner, friend, or coworker, then whatever area of my life that person infiltrated into would become reconciled and whole. The problem I soon discovered is that people are broken.

Every last one of them, myself included.

So, in the spring of 2021, I once again found myself searching for hope. This time, I didn't turn to the bottle of Moscato on the shelf, the steaming hot bath, or the new friend I had made on social media. No, my search led me to a church service and to a message I needed to hear. Instead of finding hope, hope found me. Hope found me curled up on the floor, choking back tears, begging to be seen, heard, and loved. Without pause or hesitation, hope found me. That hope was Jesus.

Instead of searching for hope in a glass of wine, a warm bath, or a new friend showing interest in me, now, I cling to the hope that Jesus freely gave me. His hope doesn't fade. It isn't circumstantial or conditional. It doesn't end in disappointment like so much hope in this world does.

The name of Jesus is the hope of the entire world. That hope is given freely to you and me. All you have to do is seek it out, and His hope will find you.

Patience is bitter, but its fruit is sweet.

Aristotle

HOPE: The Wellspring of Strength

by Sally Mary S. de Leon

*I*n the crucible of discomfort, where pain echoes in the chambers of our being, we find a poignant truth: this moment, though excruciating, is a fleeting visitor. As the ache settles in our chest and belly, radiating from head to heart, it becomes a visceral reminder of our humanity. Yet, within this storm of emotions, HOPE stands resilient, weaving a narrative that transcends the current distress.

Picture this moment as a storm passing through the vast landscape of your life. Yes, it rages with intensity, and you feel its impact at the core of your existence. But hold onto this revelation: storms and this tumult are transient. The thunderous pain and the lightning strikes of despair are elements of a passing storm. Your strength, an indomitable force, lies patiently beneath the surface, ready to emerge in the aftermath.

Amidst the chaos, let HOPE be your anchor. Breathe. Inhale the promise of renewal, exhale the residue of anguish. These breaths are not just physiological; they are whispers to your spirit, affirming endurance. In the rhythmic dance of controlled, relaxing breaths, find solace—a beacon guiding you through the storm.

Remember, the strength within you is not ephemeral; it is a perennial wellspring waiting to be tapped. This agonizing moment is but a chapter, not the entire story. As you navigate the currents of uncertainty, envision the landscape beyond this storm. Envision a future where the echoes of pain serve as stepping stones to resilience, where the scars become constellations illuminating the strength you possess.

Yes, it hurts now, but this pain is the cocoon from which your strength will gracefully emerge. In the symphony of your breath and the resilience of your spirit lies the assurance that, soon, this storm will pass. Embrace HOPE, for it is not merely a bystander but the architect of your unwritten tomorrows, where the strength within you becomes a testament to the enduring power of the human spirit.

Harmony: Find balance and unity in your pursuits;

Optimism: Embrace a hopeful and positive outlook;

Perseverance: Endure challenges with steadfast determination;

Empowerment: Strengthen yourself and others with positivity.

Choosing Hope

by Nancy Feth

*H*ave you ever wondered how some people continue to show up in life with hope and optimism, regardless of circumstances? It's as if they know something we don't, which has the power to create happiness. It is easy to compare ourselves to those around us, especially when things are not going well. However, let's examine the lifestyles of people with hope. We discover hope is a practice and a choice cultivated daily in each moment, often strengthened and nourished through relationships with self, God, and one another.

When things are going well, it is easy to have hope. There is faith in things we can see and trust in our ability to control outcomes. The challenge comes when we are faced with difficulty or uncertainty. Hope often fades as our focus shifts toward an obstacle and how to solve it. When solutions are not readily apparent, discouragement can set in. The good news is hope is found in ordinary moments shared. As we dare to share ourselves truthfully and authentically, hope inspires and can be contagious. Each of us has the potential to give and receive hope.

Take a moment to think about a challenging person or situation for you or someone you know. Allow yourself to connect with the experience. Close your eyes and get curious. Imagine you are a light of hope. How are you being? What might you say or do to encourage and shed light on the path? How can you cultivate and choose hope consistently? Take some time to act on this awareness. We become a voice for hope when we listen deeply and share our experiences, gifting one another with our presence ~ and in giving to others, we receive the gift of hope ourselves.

We should ask God to:
increase our hope when it is small,
awaken it when it is dormant,
confirm it when it is wavering,
strengthen it when it is weak,
and raise it up when it is overthrown.

John Calvin

Rising From The Fire

By Joe DiMeo

*T*here was a time when hope played a significant role in my life. There were periods when I faced multiple rejections in my life pursuits, and I felt disheartened and doubtful about my future.

Despite the setbacks, I clung to hope and continued working hard but slowly towards my goals.

One particular experience stands out vividly. It was my car accident. I was driving home from a night shift and fell asleep at the wheel. I do not even remember clocking into work. My body was engulfed in flames, burning 80% of my body.

When I woke up from three and a half month-sedated coma, the first thing I asked my mom was, "How are my rims?" I knew I was in an accident but did not know the extent of it. Though the physicians told me I was doing well, given the circumstances, learning they shaved off my hair was the most upsetting as it was a big part of my identity. Realizing they had amputated my fingertips was also devastating as I would not be able to be as independent as I was before, such as working, cooking, cleaning, or doing laundry. At 20 years old, I felt like I turned back the clock because my mom needed to help me like I was a little kid.

This experience taught me that hope can drive resilience even in the face of adversity. I am reminded daily that setbacks are not permanent, and that keeping hope can move you through anything.

Results from the accident led me to several surgeries, becoming the world's first successful face and dual hands transplant recipient. Hope has guided me as I continue to have medical procedures and face different obstacles.

Every day, I conquer tasks around the house and work towards being as independent as possible. Without hope, I would not have risen from the darkest times and continued to seek a brighter future.

When you have lost hope,
you have lost everything.
And when you think all is lost,
when all is dire and bleak,
there is always hope.

Pittacus Lore

Pain Has Purpose

Michelle Rene' Hammer

Of all the things I have learned through the years as a licensed clinical counselor, one thing has proven true time and time again. Pain takes a turn when there's purpose in it—a turn for the better. Sense from senselessness, hope to go on, and much more.

How do I know this to be true? Because it's happened to me, has happened to more patients than I count, and continues to happen now to persons I'm counseling through the hardest of times. Again and again, the pain is almost unbearable, excruciating actually, and preventing them (or back in the day, myself) from moving forward.

Until the light at the end of the tunnel appears, even if it's just a tiny crack. And the what-ifs begin. What if:

My pain matters
It is meant to help someone else.
It is a part of my destiny.
It's for something bigger.
It breaks the cycle in my family
And on and on.
I can see their wheels spinning!
It is such a huge shift the room permeates with it. The counseling room, that is. This sense of I am going to survive is palpable. So palpable you can feel it. Almost taste it. It's the taste of HOPE!

This turn of events. This facilitation of hope. This turning point, so to speak, is at the heart of what counseling is all about. Because while pain often hinders, pain with purpose propels you farther than you could ever imagine going.

So, if you are stuck, hurting, unsure how to move on, or wanna find some hope, a great way to start is this. Reach out to someone who cares, gets it, and gets you! Who will journey with you in your struggles as you grapple with the nonsense of it all? Until one day, it's not nonsense but perfectly sensible what you are going through because you've found your very own understanding of hope.

Hope is the companion of power,
and mother of success;
for who so hopes strongly has
within him the gift of miracles.

Samuel Smiles

Message of Hope - "I Want My Freedom"
by Peter Wainberg

*L*et's talk about what makes life truly special in a room filled with sunshine. People often say it's all about being happy. But, you know, sometimes we feel stuck, and it's tough to figure out why.

Think about going on a big adventure without a plan. It's like going on a trip without knowing where you want to go. Many people go through life like that—no clear plan, like a ship without a destination.

Now, let's think about having clear goals in life. It's like having a special map that shows you where to go. Having a plan isn't just about doing okay; it's like having a secret code to being really happy.

As we look closer at what makes life great, we discover something super important: the most significant thing in life is freedom. It's not just about doing whatever you want; it's also about being healthy and having enough money. This is like finding the key to a super good life.

Now, imagine telling everyone you know, "I want my freedom!" It's not just about doing well; it's about having the freedom to be healthy and have enough money. Saying these words is like opening a door to something really amazing.

This is a story about finding our way. Sometimes, it feels like we're lost in a big puzzle. But when we say, "I want my freedom," it's like turning on a light in the dark. This special message is like a big hug of hope in life. It tells us that we can have a happy and free tomorrow, and that's something super exciting for all of us.

LIFE IS TOUGH

but so

ARE YOU

Homeless to Hopeful

Christopher Rausch

As a homeless 7th-grade dropout, living in the backseat of a station wagon, surrounded by eighteen cats and four dogs, I hit rock bottom. I vividly recall feeling like there was no reason to keep going. It was a pouring rainstorm, my mother in the front seat, puffing on another cigarette, and I was quietly shedding tears. All I wanted was for the pain and misery to stop. I was starving, shivering from the cold, and the stench in that car was beyond words.

Thankfully, after enduring four unimaginably tough years on the streets, a remarkable person entered my life and breathed new hope into my weary soul. He brought light where there was only darkness and convinced me I could create new opportunities despite everything I had been through. He said, "Christopher, your potential knows no limits except those you impose on yourself!"

Looking back, I'm amazed not only by my resilience, surviving two failed suicide attempts and staring down the barrel of a gun, but also by my journey through twelve consecutive years of schooling, culminating in a master's degree the same year I bought my first house.

He provided the spark, but I had to muster every ounce of strength at the lowest point in my life to start anew. I had to believe. I had to find hope in a life that was filled with pain, abandonment, and overwhelming sadness. Without any confidence, I approached each day one step at a time, committed to taking imperfect actions, leading me to a brighter future.

With a renewed vision and the wind at my back, I shared my journey with others. At first, it was embarrassing, but the feedback inspired me to continue using my gifts to help others discover hope in their own darkness. Never give up! You will achieve whatever you set your mind to! Trust me!

AFTERWORD

Hope for Peace on Earth
by Karen Mayfield Msc. Cc

Words we speak and think about every moment of the day keep communication going. Hope is one of the words that make up our thought package — all put together in an inventory of our stories, like the stories in this book. Stories make up our spoken words. Certain words, like HOPE, are popular and used more often than others, as seen in the phrase, "I hope you like this." But isn't that the way we do everything?

When it comes to manifestation through writing, words are content fuel.

Words like HOPE are designed, one way or another, to influence people and plant positive seeds in their minds. That is what makes HOPE a target word. Hope is a highly responsive word. Hope is one of those words that can go with almost any sentence. It is a sharp indicator of where people are emotionally and how they think. Do you see and feel the word and concept of HOPE in the sentences below that have manifested hope to people since the beginning of time?

- When His peace rules our hearts, our relationships reflect His spirit of oneness. Colossians 3:15 — He is the all-ness in the nothingness. Life on earth is complete... Hope has brought us together.

- There was always hope for Humanity. We have eliminated all that is not of the plan... The call for HOPE went out, and many nations worldwide rose to answer...(*The Prohibition of Nuclear Weapons*; By: Marie Braun:...)[1] Hope has brought us together...

Life on Planet Earth and "goodwill towards men" are phrases from the Biblical annunciation to the shepherds[2] (Meridian Magazine). With HOPE, we feel words meet words because HOPE is the connector that has brought us together through word and deed, exemplified in the stories in this fantastic book. I hope you like them.

Resources:

1. https://riseuptimes.org/tag/treaty-on-the-prohibition-of-nuclear-weapons-tpnw/

2. MeridianMagazine https://latterdaysaintmag.com
https://en.wikipedia.org/wiki/Peace_on_Earth#:~:text=Peace%20on%20Earth%20may%20refer,Biblical%20annunciation%20to%20the%20shepherds

Every cloud has a silver lining.

John Milson

Front Cover
Contributing Authors

Brooke Peterson, an 'Agent for Change' in her eighth decade, says, "It's never too late to rejuvenate!" Searching for alternative solutions for health issues led her into a world of freedom and helping others create new paths to health in network marketing for over five decades. She now lives a life filled with passion, health, and excitement.

Charla Anderson Award-winning flight attendant retired. Best-selling Author. Speaker. Coach. TV/Podcast host. Ziglar Legacy Certified. Olympic Torch Bearer. Engaging podcast guest. Personal development junkie. Charla is outrageously optimistic and courageous. Joy is her lifestyle, unconditional love is her message, and mindset is her method. Entering her 7th decade with a wealth of life experience and wisdom to share. http://charlaanderson.com/

Denise C. Herndon Harvey is a best-selling author, Speaker, Transformation Coach, and Voice Actor. Denise is a Liberty University graduate with an MA in Human Service Counseling Family Advocacy. BS in Psychology – Christian Counseling, BS in Psychology – CrisisCounseling, a minor in Biblical Studies, and a Certified Life Coach.

Donna Guary is an Air Force Veteran, a Mother, Grandmother, Great Grandmother and member of the National Women in Agriculture Association. Also a children's book author, Donna's first two books in the Veggie Stories series are *"Broccoli! It's My Favorite*

Vegetable" and *"Where is the World Does Broccoli Come From?"* Both are available on Amazon.

Faith James is CEO of The Personal Branding Consultancy, LLC, and is affectionately known as the Queen of Branding. She is an award-winning branding expert and has worked on brands like IBM and Liberty Mutual. She is a 2x Int'l Amazon Best Selling Author and is currently working on her next book: God is My Brand Strategist. @faithajames on Instagram

Gin Yu was born in Taiwan, raised in Brazil, and currently living in Los Angeles, Gin Yu's journey defines her diverse identity. With a passion for telling stories, Gin balances economic acumen and creative passion as a TV and Film Producer. She is the author of "Why Am I Here?" mailto: iahtg.com

Gloria Sloan is CEO of Personal Dynamics, Inc., She is an author, professional certified life coach, and strategist. She has a passion for helping people to achieve their goals and find greater joy through self-discovery and using essential life skills. Her work focuses on transformation, ethical principles, empowerment, and personal development. Gloriasloan.com

Ilene Gottlieb is known as The Heart Healer, Ilene has been in Nursing for over 50 years and 29 years in Vibrational Healing, creating holistic approaches to clearing energy blocks and promoting healing. She has served thousands globally as an International Speaker, Vibrational Healer, and Founder of The Heart Healer Ho'oponopono Community. http://ilenethehearthealer.com/

Jessie Tieva is CEO of "Born Abel," the foundation named for her son, Abel, who was born with Trisomy 18. Born Abel features children worldwide in colorful children's books, bringing awareness to their various complex medical conditions. The Foundation runs a free baby item shelf called "Abel's Closet." Learn more at http://bornabel.com/

Kathleen (Kat) O'Keefe-Kanavos is a three-time Breast Cancer Survivor seen on Dr. Oz, The DOCTORS, NBC, CBS. She's a Video Podcaster, Columnist, WEBE Books Publisher, and award-winning Author/Lecturer who promotes patient advocacy and connecting with Inner-guidance through Dreams for success in health, wealth, and relationships. Learn more KathleenOKeefeKanavos.com

Kimberly Rinaldi, success coach, hypnotherapist, speaker, author, psychic-medium and radio show host, guides you through *Lessons in Joyful Living. Because the secret to life itself is JOY.* You'll connect with your intuition, self-healing, Divine intervention, miraculous outcomes and so much more. Join her for online events live from Southern California where she shares space with Mr. Rinaldi and their Basenji boy Jake. http://kimberlyrinaldi.com/

Mark Heidt is an award-winning writer, director, producer of $30 Million in half-hour infomercials. He has performed music at Carnegie Hall and fought forest fires in Idaho. Mark is husband to Sandy, father to Ken and Ruth, and grandfather to Graeme. His mission is to enlighten and empower. Faith is above all.

Marla Hamann is Mom to two handsome young men and a TARS Warrior Princess. She is also Grandma to a beautiful baby girl. She and Emma are the Authors of the *Emma's Adventures* Children's Book Series, encouraging others with TARS to live their best lives. Marla believes in God and "can do everything through Christ who strengthens me."

Peggy Willms has been a fitness trainer, sports nutritionist, personal and corporate health, wellness, and life coach for over thirty years. She is an entrepreneur, and multi-bestselling author (all books found on Amazon) and is a featured contributor for BizCatalyst360. She hosts The Coach Peggy Show and wellness retreats. She is a mother of two sons and a cool grandma. http://www.allthingswellness.com/ peggy@allthingswellness.com

Sally Mary DeLeon is a US Army veteran, nurse, paralegal, warrior, healer, and advocate. Mother of two and domestic violence survivor, she founded a nonprofit combating veteran homelessness. A survivor of military sexual trauma, Sally conquers daily battles of suicide ideation. VUCA trained, MindValley Evercoach Certified Life Coach — dedicated to

transforming pain into resilience, HOPE, and triumph. http://www.operationbetterme.com/

Sandra Kitt is a New Thought Ordained Minister and member of First Unity Spiritual Campus. As a proud veteran she served in the United States Army Transportation Corps. As part of her ministry Sandra started Thriving Heart Ministries and is committed to helping people overcome physical and mental disabilities. http://www.http/thrivingheartsministry.com

Tammy Hader is known as the bashful storyteller, Tammy authored *Walking Old Roads: A Memoir of Kindness Rediscovered* and she is working on the second book of her memoir series. She is an essay writer at BizCatalyst360, WebMD, Medium, the National Association of Baby Boomer Women, and Inspirations for Better Living. TammyHader.com

Will Pollock, a Native New Yorker, is an award-winning author, blogger, multimedia journalist, photographer, and creator of CrankyYank.com. Now in Midtown Atlanta, Will is a permaculture and green-living evangelist and lifelong tennis player. As the world's proudest papa to Cam, his new children's book, *Gentle with Gertie*, is a story of human-and-furry siblings, available on Amazon.

Contributing Authors

A lan Jude Summa is an internationally published illustrator & author. He began drawing at age two and never stopped. Alan has two children and lives in Poconos with his wife, Laura, two cats, two dogs, and a lizard named, Doc. When not working, he loves to travel and restore vintage motorcycles.

Alysia Lyons is a mom, entrepreneur, life coach and author. She is passionate about helping women live their lives with more joy, from the inside out. As a certified Master Neuro-Transformational Life Coach, Alysia guides her clients to emotional freedom. Her blog, the Mom Support Coach, focuses on lessons she learns in daily life. www.alysialyons.com info@alysialyons.com

Amanda Gust is the co-founder and President of Born Abel, a non-profit dedicated to celebrating the worth and humanity of children born with complex medical needs. She enjoys spending time with her family, volunteering at her church, and cheering on her five children in their various sports and activities. Amanda@BornAbel.com

Andrew Foster's words serves as bridges, connecting cultures and ideologies. His poetic diplomacy in essence, is an extension of his poetic endeavor, where he seeks to mend the tears in the fabric of humanity globally with the same empathy and artistry that characterizes his poetic ethos for change.

Angi Currier is a best-selling author and medical Patient Access Representative. She has three children and a granddaughter. She hopes to inspire others with her triumph over addiction. Angi feels like she has lived two lives. The first life involves physical and emotional struggles, and the second is living in gratitude, acceptance, and confidence. ajhinkle5@yahoo.com

Beth Goodman, Dr. is a Visionary, Entrepreneur, Speaker, Breast Cancer SurTHRIVER, and life Advancement Coach. Her mission is to cultivate confidence in women to accept themselves in God's image. She believes that confidence should not be a difficult goal but a fundamental aspect of everyday life.

Beth Johnston is the oldest daughter in a large family; Beth Johnston was born into management! Beth has spent her professional years reorganizing existing companies using her practical and logical perspectives to help companies achieve their highest profit years. She is known for her keen listening skills and inspiring interview techniques, now shared on B.E.P. TALKS. Beth can be reached http:// info@beptalks.com

Bonita Joy bring the experience of joy to your events through speaking and emceeing. Her witty ventriloquism puppets pop up to surprise and delight your attendees. Her forthcoming book is "Tickle Their Funny Bone: Use Humor to Polish Your Presentations." *For a complimentary Humor Journal* go to https://joy.funandfunnier.com BonitaJoySpeaker@gmail.com

Brenda Warren, The Soulutionist, is a Retired Marine with over three decades of experience in leadership, self-care, spiritual growth, and cultivating healthy relationships. Three-time best-selling author, pattern for living, and self-publishing coach. Brenda has helped countless individuals transform their lives using her innovative TAPIN Method™ (Transformation Announce Prepare Imagine Nurture). https://linktr.ee/brendathesoulutionist

Carolyn Ballenger has been a Unity Truth student for over 30 years and a Chaplain for over 15 years. Ordained through www.illli.org, she is a New Thought Minister who has studied 7 World Religions, A Course in Miracles, Mastermind, and Science of Mind. Carolyn loves to rhyme; see her collaborations at http://www.firstunity.org/

Christopher Crouse is a true Renaissance man. He is a business owner, minister, and writer/author. He loves teaching and performing drama, painting and drawing, singing, and playing the bass guitar. Most importantly, he loves Jesus, his wife Jenn, children, and grandchildren. http://Chris@ChrisCrouse.com

Christopher Rausch is an author and debatably the world's most effective and impactful UNSTOPPABLE "No Excuses" coach, speaker, workshop facilitator, and retreat leader. With a Master's Degree in Organizational Management and over 30+ years of experience, he has personally and professionally applied his education and life experiences to build a thriving coaching business. Catch his RAW & UNSCRIPTED Show on YouTube.

Cyndi Wilkins is a certified massage and bodywork professional with a passion for writing/blogging and blazing new trails of thinking. Her approach to healing is recognizing the mind and body function as ONE. She is a bestselling author, featured contributor for *Bizcatalyst 360* and guest blogger for *All Things Wellness*

Debra Costanzo founded 3 in 1 Fitness by D. L. Costanzo, LLC in July 2008. Certified through the Institute of Integrative Nutrition, she loves coaching busy professionals and supporting them to embrace mindful lifestyle changes resulting in better health and sustained energy. Debra resides in Charlotte, North Carolina. http://debracostanzo@3in1fitness.com

Dennis J. Pitocco is the founder of 360° Nation, created over a decade ago with the sole purpose of rediscovering humanity at its best. Everything is done "for good" versus for profit. It's comprised of Biz-Catalyst 360°, an award-winning publishing platform, 360° Nation Studios, a multi-media enterprise, and GoodWorks 360°, a pro bono consulting foundation for nonprofits worldwide. bizmastersglobal@gmail.com http://www.bizcatalyst360.com/author/dennisjpitocco/

Eileen Bild is the CEO and Executive Producer at OTELproductions, ROKU Channel Developer and Talk Show host for OTEL TALK. She is an author and internationally syndicated columnist for BizCatalyst360, Life Coaching Magazine, Women's Voice Magazine, and NSAEN. She is also a Breakthrough S.P.A.R.K. Coach. https://linktr.ee/eileenbild

Fran Asaro is a Virtual Partner, helping entrepreneurs start and grow their business. She is the founder of the Senior Tuber Community, where she helps mature people share their legacy and gifts by teaching them how to become YouTube Content Creators. https://www.thriveanyway.com/   https://www.youtube.com/@FranAsaro/featured Schedule a call with Fran https://calendly.com/seniortuber/30_minute_meet_fran_youtube_call

Gina Lobito is a Transformational Coach, Energy Intuitive with a background in Bodywork, Shamanism, Healing Arts. Gina facilitated Full Moon Drum Circles and began her journey into the healing power of the drum and sound. She has advanced studies in Self Mastery which lead her to create Soul-Inspired to guide others through their transformation and Ascension Process. She has worked in Law Enforcement and hosts a radio show, has sheepadoodle, loves the beach, and lives in California.

Ida Ra Nalbandian, is the author of *Does God Have a Bicycle* and *Jacob's Magic Vegetables*. She and her family founded VSCF: Vahagn Setian Charitable Foundation, in memory of her late son, promotes self-awareness and mindful choices. *Jacob's Magic Vegetables* is a tribute to the expansion of the greater good.

Jack Rehill currently serves as assistant pastor at harvest church in northeastern Pennsylvania where he has served in that capacity for nearly 24 years. He and his wife Patricia have been married for 52 years. He is the author of a recently released book entitled, "The Advocate and the adversary."

Jacki Long, B.A. psychology, is a Certified Jack Canfield Success Principles Trainer. Mentored by Sean Smith for over 10 years, Jacki is certified in Neurolinguistic Programming (NLP) and a featured trainer for advanced coaching certification courses. Jacki customizes programs for clients, helping them achieve their highest personal and professional goals. coachjacklong@gmail.com

Janice Silva dreams big and brings others along. An entrepreneur and travel lover, Janice lives in Maui with her husband of 25 years. They wanted to live where the bougainvillea always blooms and have been blessed to do so. Janice offers Wellness Concierge services in Maui, Mexico, and Central California. http://joyfulmauiwellness.com./

Jeniece Paige is the Founder and CEO of Black Vegan Health & Wellness Enterprise and The Foundation of Get Ready 4 The Dress Podcast (GR4TD). She's a certified Nutrition, Personal Trainer, and Life Coach. Jeniece is currently working on her PhD in Holistic and Sports Nutrition. www.linktr.ee/bvfitness

Jodie Fitzgerald is a Licensed Family Dog Mediator ®, owner of Fitz Your Dog Training and a former nurse. After working with rescue for five years, she is dedicated to educating dog lovers about the dogs' truth and creating amazing relationships that will keep dogs in homes with their families.

Joe DiMeo is the world's first successful face and double-hand transplant recipient. At the age of 20, a tragic car accident left Joe with 3rd degree burns over 80% of his body, and he spent 3.5 months in a coma. After ten months on a donor list, Joe beat the odds and found a donor. There was only a 6% chance of a match. Joe is an avid proponent of organ, blood, and tissue donors. He lives in New Jersey with his girlfriend and their beloved dogs, Kirkland and Buster.

Johnny Tan is an Experiential Keynote Speaker, Executive Career and Life Coach, Mentor, Multi-Award-Winning and Bestselling Author, Talk Show Host, Social Entrepreneur, Founder and CEO of From My Mama's Kitchen®, and Words Have Power store, Publisher of "Inspirations for Better Living" digital magazine, and a REIKI Master Teacher and Healer.

Katerina Pappas was born in Philadelphia and grew up in Athens, Greece. She is a licensed attorney, author, and soon to be kundalini yoga instructor. Her passions are cooking, writing children's books, and long impromptu walks. Her dream is to help others re-awaken the divine wisdom of their bodies.

Lara Scriba loves exploring new places, and whether she's sailing the world with her family or discovering the nuances of her inner world, her curiosity always leads her to look just below the surface. Her passion to support others to heal through a holistic lens has been

nurtured by her background in nursing, work as a Reiki practitioner, Yoga Teacher specializing in stress resilience, ayurvedic habits and eating disorder recovery, and Numerologist. k2kyoga@gmail.com www.kitokaizenyoga.com

Laura Fleming Summa career began in Commercial Art and advertising. She transitioned to illustrating. She is currently Vice President at Leadbelly Productions, a creative think tank producing products and services for children. Laura is married to Alan Jude Summa, also an artist. Together, they raised two grown children, and all reside in Northeast Pennsylvania.

Linda B. Kaye pushed through tough times to become a digital marketing agency owner. To get there, she combined seemingly unrelated education and job skills. She is a U.S. Army Veteran with an MBA and Marketing Certificate from Southern NH University. Linda started working with computers in the early 1970s as technology was emerging. https://interactivesynergy.com/

Lisa Caroglanian Dorazio's is a bestselling author and speaker. Her contributions appear globally in newspapers, magazines, and trade publications, and her co-authored book Conversations that Make a Difference: Stories Supporting a Bigger Vision. Embracing a servant mindset, Lisa founded CanAmeri Consulting, Inc. to always be a "Difference Maker" in the lives of others. www.canamericonsulting.com

Lucia Murphy was born and raised in Scranton, PA. Lucia is a pianist, loves to travel, and listens to music all over the world. She loves

her husband Glynn, and stepchildren, Glynn Jr, Amanda, and Hallie, very much next to own mother, Assunta, brother John, and niece Lena Maria. https://linktr.ee/LuciaandGlynn

M Moses Andradé was born in Kingston, Jamaica, West Indies, and served as a pastor for twenty-five years. He is pursuing a career as a professional voice actor and visual artist. Moses also sings Sacred Classical music regularly for church choirs and choral ensembles as a bass soloist. https://m.soundcloud.com/voiceartmusic63

Mark Nelson O'Brien is the principal of O'Brien Communications Group https://obriencg.com/ a B2B brand-management and marketing firm he founded in 2004. He's also the co-founder and President of EinSource. And he's a lifelong writer. You can see all of his published work on Amazon.

Markus Wettstein. M.D. has practiced endocrinology for thirty years. He is a diabetes, metabolic and stress management specialist. He also works in energy medicine as a Licensed Bio-Well practitioner. He assists clients in improving their health and wellness by measuring their energy field, stress level, health status, and energy reserve via electro photonic imaging. mwettst@gmail.com

Martareisa Logue is grateful for life's blessings, She embraces her limb difference. Diverse experiences, from gymnastics to soccer and leadership roles, shaped her. Martareisa's unaltered hands tell a unique story, guided by faith. Her journey will inspire you to embrace your uniqueness and overcome adversity with unwavering strength and belief in your potential. For more detailed and up-to-date information about Thrombocytopenia-absent radius (TAR) Syndrome, I recommend visiting the following websites: TAR Syndrome Awareness Texas NCBI Bookshelf - TAR Syndrome

Maxine Tomlinson is the CEO and Founder of The Metanoia Life She is a Kingdom woman who openly declares her love for God. She is an artist who draws her inspiration from Biblical themes and stories and considers her artwork as prophetic in nature. She is a devoted mother and grandmother.

Melanie Soloway is the Founder and Co-Director of Raising Enlightened Children and a master certified Life Coach who has taught parenting for over 20 years. Melanie is the mother of three children. She believes that learning positive parenting tools, and how to apply them and understanding our programming is critical to becoming the best parent and person we can be. http://raisingenlightened-children.com/

Melody Dixon is the CEO and Founder of Pro Event Planners Creators Eco-Focused Events. This daughter of Jamaica is very passionate about encouraging and uplifting women and little girls. She enjoys gardening and being out in nature. As such she has found a way to infuse that in her business. Www.MyProEventPlanners.com

Michelle Rene' Hammer, MS, LCPC, a Certified Pastoral Counselor, BREAKTHROUGH Coach, motivational speaker, bestselling author, and host of *Breakthrough Today with Michelle Rene'* helps women

leaders navigate life's challenges in clinical and biblical ways. Her mission is to empower successful yet overextended Christian women to break through barriers to satisfying relationships and abundant joy-filled lives. http://thevchc.org/

Nancy Feth is a strategic catalyst for authentic connection and positive relationships. Passionate about community building, business development, leadership, and entrepreneurship, Nancy's current focus is creating positive, dynamic, results-oriented sales teams that deliver customer-centric, best-in-class services and experiences within a culture of collaboration, integrity, and innovation. http://nancyafeth@gmail.com

Patricia Dolce is a published author of a successful children's book and contributing author to additional publications. Patricia taught Preschool, Kindergarten children, and religious education and is now retired. She is a past member of a local women's club and is actively involved with the homeowners' association as a member of several committees.

Peter Wainberg is an international speaker, author, educator, and life coach specializing in Heart Health and Self-Love and helping people to have the freedom to live their healthiest and happiest lives. His **Heart Health Mastery** course shares secrets he discovered while transforming his heart health. mailto:info@freedomland.comhttp://www.myhearthandbook.com/

Robyn Drothler, MED CCC-SLP, author of ABCs of Speech, is the owner of Advantage Speech Therapy Services, a mobile-based speech therapy company in the Milton, Ga area - EST in 2004. She works 1:1 with children of varying diagnoses to help them learn to communicate. https://advantagespeech.com/author/robyn-drothler/

Rhonda Douglas Charles is the immigrant career strategist and founder of Adnohr Docs in Brooklyn, NY, who champions professional growth for 1st and 2nd-generation immigrants. With 25+ years of providing career services, she has guided everyone from new grads to top execs. An immigrant herself, Rhonda's mission is to ease the transformation from survival jobs to thriving careers.

Sandra (Sandy) Heidt is a retired teacher and coach of St. Petersburg High School, Florida's champion swim and track teams. She is an avid scrapbooker, mother to daughter Ruth, son Kenneth, and grandmother to Graeme. Sandy and her college sweetheart husband, Mark, have been married for 48 years.

Shantay Adams is a dynamic light firehouse Speaker, Author with a Transformation & Empowering program. In addition, she provides Consulting services and is a License Minister by grace through faith. As a servant in heart and an influential leader, her purpose is to serve others with sound wisdom and counsel.

Sharlene R Prince is an Author, and Overcoming Strategist/The Queen of Possibilities, where she strongly believes there is a solution to every dilemma. She works with Survivors of Domestic Violence, to help them restructure and rebuild their lives. She assists people in finding a way to overcome the storms in Life, as they forge forward. Her Royalty Mindset Elevation Strategic programs works to develop the Riches in You, so your mindset can change your perspective in Life. Mother of three and Mentor for the Masses. Sharlene has a master's in human resource and development from Barry University.

Sharon Durbin Graves has always been creative, but an artist emerged from within me 22 years ago. She paints daily in acrylics and teaches painting classes in person and online. Sharon specializes in teaching beginners. Her YouTube channel is Beginning Acrylic Teacher, and her website is www.paintingwithacrylics101.com slgraves6@gmail.com

Sonia Waite is a wife, mom, and business owner and operates a home-based foodservice business in Markham, Ontario. Sonia's creations include delicious baked treats and freshly arranged fruit, veggie, and charcuterie platters for people who enjoy serving artisanal tasty treats made with traditional methods and contains high quality ingredients, and lots of love when gathering with their loved ones. You can taste love in every bite! Sewcreate21@gmail.com

Sophia Long is a scholar studying sociology and women, gender, and sexuality studies at IUPUI. She is an avid activist and intersectional feminist, currently living in the Midwest with her partner and two cats. sophialongwrites@gmail.com

Sylvie Plante is a former Human Resources Sr. Director with over 40 years of international experience in the Software, Engineering, and Professional Services industries. She holds accreditations and certifications in Leadership. She teaches Human Resources at the University level and coaches individuals who want to get to the next level and reinvent themselves. http://Sylvie.plante@createalify-bydesign.com http://www.sylvie-plante.com/

Tanner Willms is a bestselling author, logistics specialist and spent six years in the oil and gas industry as an NDT inspector. He and his wife, Brittney, have two sons, Crew and Dutton. twillms79@gmail.com

Tiffany Murphy loves missions, people, and ministry owns the online retail store *Gifts By Tiffany Murphy* and Evangelist Murphy founded the Daughters of Esther, an online prayer group for women. She enjoys helping people create a healthy lifestyle God's way.

While there's life, there's hope.

Marcus Tullius Cicero

Meet the Author
Teresa Velardi

*T*eresa is a bestselling author, publisher, host of the *Conversations That Make a Difference* podcast, coach, and potter.

Michelangelo, the famous 15th-century artist and sculptor said, *Every block of stone has a statue inside it, and it is the sculptor's task to discover it.* His job was to remove the excess stone to reveal the beauty within.

Similarly, Teresa uses the art of pottery to illustrate that each ball of clay can and will be transformed into a beautiful work of art with the touch of the potter's hand. Teresa guides her clients through the process of centering, molding, shaping, and walking through the fire of challenges to effect positive life change as they gracefully and powerfully embrace the work of art they already are.

Teresa found her passion and purpose through life's challenges while trusting God's plan. Faith in God, gratitude, and giving are her heart. Her abilities as a writer, editor, and publisher are vital ingredients she brings to those who share their message with the world on her podcast or through her publishing platform.

Her daily quiet time, writing, and gratitude practice keep Teresa focused on her God-given purpose as life unfolds in this ever-changing world. We all have a story to tell and a heartfelt message to share. What's your message?

https://linktr.ee/teresavelardi

Meet the Foreword
Vincent A. Lanci

Vincent A. Lanci has dedicated his life to normalizing the conversation around mental health and inspiring entrepreneurship. After graduating with degrees in Bachelor of Science in Finance and Master of Business Administration, becoming a published author was not always the plan. After surviving a near-death hit-and-run accident while on foot, he had two choices: sit and sulk, or make a difference. Vincent in an International multi-best-selling author, speaker, and Top 1% podcaster.

Vincent passions outside of work are to speak with students using my books, exercise, and watch my favorite sports teams. Vincent enjoys his role as a Big Brother in Big Brothers Big Sisters and on the Tampa General Hospital Patient and Family Advisory Board.

Meet the Afterword
Karen Mayfield

*K*aren is a CTA-certified coach, Metaphysical Minister, creator of the Peace of Mind Principles Coaching program, co-creator, and publisher of the Wake up Women book series.

Karen is a former Mars Venus facilitator, and relationship coach and Wake up Women's co-creator. She also created You've Got Prayer, a global prayer link for peace, harmony, hope, and gratitude.

Utilizing the Laws of Attraction in thought, clarity, and action, Karen now lives a life she loves. Being a mom, grandmother, friend, and member of a family of Entrepreneurial women is the inspiration behind Karen's purpose. "When you help women, you help the world." Life experiences have provided Karen with the wisdom needed to assist others in living a life they love.

Hope Story Take-Aways

Name of Story:

Author:

How I connected to the Story:

Hope Story Take-Aways

Name of Story:

Author:

How I connected to the Story:

Hope Story Take-Aways

Name of Story:

Author:

How I connected to the Story:

Hope Story Take-Aways

Name of Story:

Author:

How I connected to the Story:

Hope Story Take-Aways

Name of Story:

Author:

How I connected to the Story:

Hope Story Take-Aways

Name of Story:

Author:

How I connected to the Story:

Hope Story Take-Aways

Name of Story:

Author:

How I connected to the Story:

Daily Gift Book Series

The Daily Gift Book Series Continues:

Coming Soon

Daily Gift of Kindness
A Daily Gift of Happiness
Daily Gift of Friendship
Daily Gift of Peace

Do you have a story for one of the
next books in the series?

Learn how you can
be a contributing author at:

DailyGiftBookSeries.com

Made in the USA
Las Vegas, NV
12 November 2024

11708105R00127